HITCHCOCK ANNUAL
2015

Hitchcock

2015

Editors
Sidney Gottlieb and Richard Allen

Editorial Advisory Board
Charles Barr   Thomas L. Leitch
James Naremore   David Sterritt
Michael Walker

Founding Editor
Christopher Brookhouse

Editorial Associate
Renata Jackson

Cover Design
Deborah Dutko

We evaluate manuscripts for the *Hitchcock Annual* throughout the year. Send any correspondence by mail to Sidney Gottlieb, Department of Communication and Media Studies, Sacred Heart University, 5151 Park Avenue, Fairfield, Connecticut 06825. Send submissions by e-mail to spgottlieb@aol.com

We invite articles on all aspects of Hitchcock's life, works, and influence, and encourage a variety of critical approaches, methods, and viewpoints. For all submissions, follow the guidelines of the *Chicago Manual of Style*, using full notes rather than works cited format. We prefer submissions by e-mail, in any standard word processing format, which makes it easier to circulate essays for editorial review. The responsibility for securing any permissions required for publishing material in the essay rests with the author. Illustrations may be included, but as separate TIFF files rather than as part of the text file. Decision time is normally within three months. The submission of an essay indicates your commitment to publish it, if accepted, in the *Hitchcock Annual*, and that it is not simultaneously under consideration for publication elsewhere.

For all orders, including back issues, contact Columbia University Press, 61 West 62nd Street, New York, NY 10023; www.columbia/edu/cu/cup

The *Hitchcock Annual* is indexed in the *Film Literature Index* and *MLA International Bibliography*.

♛ Columbia University Press   *New York*

Columbia University Press
Publishers Since 1893
New York   Chichester, West Sussex

Copyright © 2016 Sidney Gottlieb/*Hitchcock Annual*
All rights reserved

ISBN 978-0-231-17619-4 (pbk. : alk. paper)
ISSN 1062-5518

∞

Columbia University Press books are printed on
permanent and durable acid-free paper.
This book is printed on paper with recycled content.

Printed in the United States of America

p 10 9 8 7 6 5 4 3 2 1

References to Internet Web sites (URLs) were accurate at the
time of writing. Neither the editors nor Columbia University
Press are responsible for URLs that may have expired or
changed since the manuscript was prepared

AMY SARGEANT

Hitchcock's Easy Virtue in Context

"Being modern only means twisting things into different shapes." —Noël Coward, *Easy Virtue* (1927)[1]

In the following essay I intend to discuss Hitchcock's *Easy Virtue* (released July 1927) in the context of a number of contemporaneous and preceding renditions, in film and fiction, of the "older woman" and "the gigolo." Noël Coward's source text "twisted" an old theme for a modern audience, and Hitchcock, in turn, exerted further idiosyncratic "twists" in bringing the play to the screen. This is not to say that Isabel Jeans (1891-85), who plays Larita Filton in the film, is significantly older than Robin Irvine (1901-33), who plays John Whittaker, but that the presentation of wealthy divorcee Larita as "a woman with a past" whose second husband is conspicuously younger than her first is crucial to Hitchcock's transformation of Coward's play. Larita—who explicitly acknowledges the age difference in the play—is perceived and presented as older by way of experience by Hitchcock and a fear that John may be perceived as an emasculated "silly boy"—or even worse, a pathetic gigolo—shadows some of the bitter opposition to their marriage. I am also interested in the ways in which Hitchcock, here as elsewhere, provides a critique of the role of the media, especially newspapers and magazines, in circulating images of and stories about these characters, inciting an audience and affecting reputation and social standing.[2] In general I urge that *Easy Virtue* be re-viewed in the context of British culture of the 1920s, still much lacking in Hitchcock commentary.

Figure 1

Personnel, Themes, and
the Hitchcockian Elements of Easy Virtue

For audiences in 1927, Jeans was as much in the public eye as Larita, as likely to be encountered on the fashion and society pages of newspapers as in stage and screen reviews. In 1925, "The best-dressed star of the British screen" appeared in ads for Ciro Pearls and in 1927 could be spotted modeling hats for Marshall and Snelgrove.[3] (fig 1) In *Easy Virtue*'s early flashback sequence, Larita sits for an eminent society

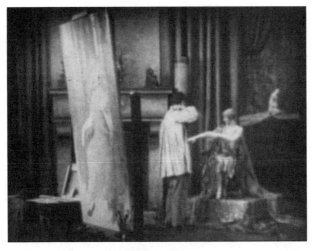

Figure 2

portraitist, Claude Robson (Eric Bransby-Williams), who
hopes to relieve her of the boorish and jealous drunkard Mr.
Filton (Franklin Dyall): "I'd give everything in the world to
make you happy," he writes to Larita, prior to Filton's assault
on Claude, Larita's surprising comforting of Filton, Claude's
supposed consequent suicide and Filton's divorce of Larita.
The sequence shows Larita's portrait in progress, with Claude
working on a canvas that leans toward rather than away from
him (fig. 2). Larita is throughout, as Thomas Leitch has
observed, the object of public gaze and scrutiny, framed and
placed in focus.[4] Audience familiarity with Jeans's previous
and concurrent stage and screen roles, most presciently on
stage in the 1924 Ivor Novello and Constance Collier play, *The
Rat*, revived on stage in 1927 and directed on film by Graham
Cutts in 1925, further inflects a reading of *Easy Virtue* as an
"older woman" scenario.

Irvine, meanwhile, was perennially cast as "the boy," as
Larita, indeed, refers to him in Hitchcock's film. He was cast
in 1925 as Simon Bliss (making his first appearance "in an
extremely dirty tennis shirt and baggy grey flannels') in
Coward's *Hay Fever*, at the Ambassadors."[5] And in *Downhill*

Figure 3

(released May 1927, and retitled in the USA as *When Boys Leave Home*), he plays Tim Wakeley, the vicar's son whose honor is protected by Roddy (Ivor Novello), his roommate and potentially Captain of the School, the only son of Sir Thomas Berwick. Roddy, Tim's accomplice in the rendezvous connived by a scheming, flirtatious sometime school waitress (Annette Benson)—"I Want Some Money" is the disc she portentously plays in the back room of the Derbyshire "Ye Olde Bunne Shoppe"—is confronted by his headmaster and squarely shoulders the blame for Tim's mishap, while Tim's shoulders droop.[6] In *Downhill*, Isabel Jeans is cast as Julia, a much-powdered, coiffured, and groomed actress, who, with her equally pampered partner (Ian Hunter), jowls and frown lines eased, proceeds to divest ingenue Roddy of a recently inherited fortune of £30,000, with the sum reiterated in the film's intertitles. Julia taunts Roddy: "Why, you silly boy, I believe you're falling in love with me," which he apparently foolishly does (and of which foolishness her partner, purposefully feigning boredom, was connivingly aware and in which complicit, Julia and her slipped cigarette case simply serving as bait). The marriage of this "Famous Actress" to

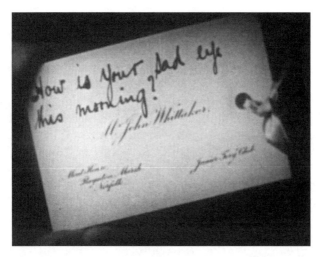

Figure 4

Roddy Berwick is duly announced by way of a newspaper insert, with Roddy subsequently acknowledging his mistake. Similarly, in Graham Cutts's *Confetti* (released December 1927), its action set against the Nice Carnival, Irvine is cast as Carlo (again appearing alongside Annette Benson) and is dissuaded by his aunt from an attachment to an older woman in favor of a more appropriate, younger prospect. Larita, in *Easy Virtue*, is essentially innocent (like the falsely accused and doubly compromised Roddy in *Downhill*) yet presumed guilty on account of her magnetic charm. (She is far from "Grey," the alias behind which she seeks to hide herself from attention in the Riviera hotel register.) Larita is pursued by a nobleman, who sends flowers and a card expressing his "undying admiration," but Hitchcock confirms her disinterest in social status by showing her preference for a more worthy suitor, John, whose card conveys real concern for her after she had been accidentally struck by a tennis ball (figs. 3 and 4).

I am particularly interested in how narratives in 1920s British cinema accommodate characters who, literally or metaphorically, make a spectacle of themselves or have spectacularity thrust upon them. Excessive spectacularity may disrupt narrative flow and serve simultaneously as a marker of social transgression. In *Easy Virtue*, the attention Larita draws is often unwanted—she hides her face with her hands before hurling a book at a camera sitting on a shelf in John's parental home.[7] As Michael Williams has noted, Larita is haunted by the memory of the flashing cameras that attended the opening court case, taunted by the sight of the camera, representing "the literal picturing of the past . . . the means by which . . . events can return to "expose" her."[8] Significantly, Mrs. Whittaker (Violet Farebrother), unlike the Riviera hotel guests who instantly recognize slandered Larita as "notorious," is prompted at second-hand to recall the circumstances of her previous sighting of Larita, by way of photographs: the splashy spread covering the polo match in the *Tatler* prompts her discovery of the portrait of Larita reported on and pictured in the same society magazine rather than via her direct inquisition regarding "mutual friends" or at the polo match itself—or via marginal legal entries in *The Times* (which are relatively small in Hitchcock's film but feature incriminatingly large in Coward). Denying Larita's accusation of betrayal, the plaintiff's barrister (Ian Hunter) appointed at her first divorce, coincidentally a guest at the same polo match and ensuing Moat House party, swears to her that he has said nothing, but that "it was bound to come out—you can't hide a thing like that." Famously, at the very end, Larita directly addresses the stalking cameramen who attend a markedly deserted courtroom for her second divorce: "Shoot—there's nothing left to kill."[9]

I should also like to counter the criticism made, not least by Hitchcock's contemporaries, that *Easy Virtue* is a film that "had no Hitchcock,"[10] by noting its flashes of Hitchcockian humor (as also in *Downhill* and *The Lodger* [1926]): shots of a French poodle surrounded by swanky "Blue Train" valises and then a British bulldog accompanied by milk churns summarily denoting a lengthy journey; a drowsy carriage driver and two nuzzling horses rudely interrupted by an impatient motorist; a memorable eavesdropping telephone operator (Benita Hume) miming a mini-drama as she

Figure 5

presumably overhears the acceptance of the wedding proposal (fig. 5); and in the midst of a domestic crisis, a servant proffering a choice of curiously bizarre Japanese lanterns, as per Coward, to whom Larita responds with demonstrative composure.[11] As in *Blackmail* (1929), unchaperoned visits to an artist's studio have disastrous consequences. As Brill has observed, there is a consciousness of class in *Easy Virtue* which is matched in *The Lodger* and asserted horribly in *The Skin Game* (1931).[12] There is also Hitchcockian irony (Mrs. Whittaker's venomous and prurient desire to be shocked is duly rewarded by her discovery of Larita's "vile secret") and the presence in Mrs. Whittaker of what Leitch calls "maleficent" and Brill terms "terrible" and "vicious" mother figures.[13] Farebrother, as the upper middle-class Mrs. Whittaker, takes her cue from Coward:

> The stern repression of any sex emotions all her life has brought her to middle age with a faulty digestion which doesn't so much sour her temper as spread it. She views the world with the jaundiced eyes of a

woman who subconsciously realizes she has missed
something, which means in point of fact that she has
missed everything.[14]

Mrs. Whittaker presumes—wrongly—that Larita is an
adventuress who has "pitchforked" herself into a family in
order to gain social position. As in Coward, Hitchcock's Mrs.
Whittaker is also a hypocrite. An intertitle notes that she
makes "Larita's life a burden to her—in private . . . But she
was all smiles and sweetness with her—in public." At the
Moat House party, she advises her daughters to behave "as
nothing unusual had happened." Larita (Jeans's calmness
here is cued by Coward's text and Jane Cowl's performance in
the play on stage) responds with as much self-restraint as she
can summon, reserving the expression of her distress for the
privacy of her bedroom.

Furthermore, as Steve Jacobs persuasively argues, there
is much in *Easy Virtue* which presages subsequent
Hitchcock films:

Hitchcock's hostile mothers are invariably linked to
the home and, consequently, to domestic architecture.
In addition, *Easy Virtue* contains another typical
Hitchcock pattern that relates to the tensions within
the family and the house: after an elided honeymoon
sequence, there is a post-honeymoon scene that shows
that things are beginning to go wrong, as in *Downhill*,
Rebecca [1940]and *Suspicion* [1941].[15]

As in *Rebecca*, a new wife wishes that she could return from
stifling parochial England to happier honeymoon days on the
French Riviera (Mandelay is archaic and aristocratic; the Moat
House is, perhaps, excessively gothicky Gothic with its frieze
of saints hovering ominously over the dining room).[16]

The dramatic use of a staircase, destined to become a
typical Hitchcockian motif (as in *Rebecca*, where an arrival at a
party goes horribly wrong for the second Mrs. de Winter),
here corresponds to Coward's original directions for the

Figure 6

country house setting and the London staging of his play (fig. 6)—as did Hitchcock's direction from the stage version of *The Lodger*. The barrage of press photographers by which a female protagonist is confronted on her departure from court finds its most obvious echo in *Notorious* (1946).

Easy Virtue *on Stage*

Basil Dean, to whom Coward dedicated *Easy Virtue*, secured the British and American production rights to the play and Coward's singular Ruritanian venture, *The Queen Was in the Parlour* (originally titled *Nadya*) in 1924.[17] *Easy Virtue* opened, accessorized by Parisian frocks, in New York in November 1925, before transferring to Manchester as "A New Play by Noël Coward," then to London's Duke of York's with the American, Jane Cowl, reprising to great acclaim her defining role as Larita:

> She has no devastating prettiness; her features are a battle-ground for the emotions rather than a lawn for garden-party simpering. . . . This actress has poise, and pace, and she delivers the second-act tirade as such things ought to be delivered, while her sullens at the end are magnificent. Miss Cowl acts with her

whole body and her gestures are expressive enough to convey meaning to anybody who should know no English. She has that style which is almost a physical quality, understanding and temperament. Finally, she possesses what the French call "le *la* du rôle."[18]

In 1927, *Easy Virtue* toured the provinces.[19] Jeans, on screen, proved herself an equally flamboyant match for Cowl, on stage: as noted in a 1929 review, "Nobody can play these hard, glittering, beautiful women with the same air as Miss Jeans."[20] Christine Gledhill reports that *Easy Virtue* was originally intended for direction on screen by Cutts, but that it was instead offered by Michael Balcon to Hitchcock.[21] With Cutts as screenwriter, *The Queen Was in the Parlour* (released April 1927) became, like *Easy Virtue*, a story opening with a wife abused by a boorish, violent, and drunkard husband. While *The Sketch* applauded *Easy Virtue* on stage as "A Cowl and Coward Success," the *Daily Film Renter* meanwhile suggested that the combination of Cutts, Coward and Lili Damita in *The Queen Was in the Parlour*, a Gainsborough/UFA co-production, "should draw large crowds."[22] However, other critics, and Balcon himself, retrospectively, thought that silent cinema failed to do justice to Coward's unique flair for wittily sharp and brisk repartee.[23] In other words, *Easy Virtue* on screen could be construed as a Coward adaptation with not enough Coward in it while simultaneously being criticized as insufficiently Hitchcockian.

Sourcing and Contextualizing Easy Virtue:
Preceding and Contemporaneous Plays and Novels

Noël Coward, by his own admission, wrote the play *Easy Virtue* (deemed by Rohmer and Chabrol merely "shallow" but appraised more sympathetically by Leitch) in celebration of a splendid type of woman "with a past" whom he thought was then disappearing from the stage.[24] "My object in writing it," he recalled in his autobiography, "had been primarily to adapt a story, intrinsically Pinero in theme and structure, to present-day behavior, to compare the *declassé* woman of today with the more flamboyant *demi-mondaine* of the nineties."[25] Elsewhere he noted that:

> It is easy nowadays to laugh at these vanished moral attitudes but they were poignant enough in their time because they were true. . . . The narrow-mindedness, the moral righteousness and the over-rigid social codes have disappeared but with them has gone much that was graceful, well-behaved and endearing. It was in a mood of nostalgic regret at the decline of such conventions that I wrote *Easy Virtue*.[26]

A less celebratory impression of the "older woman" is given in the opportunistic "modern day" conclusion of Coward's later *Cavalcade* (1932).[27] Conversely, in the former category, actually *declassé*, one might care to consider Violet Trefusis, whose tempestuous affair with the Bohemian Vita Sackville-West ended in 1923; in the latter, one might place Violet's mother, Mrs. Keppel, a *demi-mondaine* socially received as mistress of the Prince of Wales.[28] Amongst contemporaneous, congenial, fictitious counterparts, Coward was probably thinking of Michael Arlen's hugely successful *The Green Hat: A Romance for a Few People* (1924), drawing, in part, on the real-life exploits of Idina Sackville. The novel was staged in 1925 with Tallulah Bankhead, dressed by Chanel, as the notorious Iris Storm, "the poor shameless, shameful lady," who ultimately heroically proves herself honorable.[29] He may also have had in mind the crimson-hatted Priscilla in Arlen's "Confessions of a Naturalised Englishman":

> But away with hats, green or crimson, and let us get back to the delicious moment when Priscilla swept into the Mont Agel, bringing with her the gold of the sun and a profound contempt for the Conservative Party, the usages of society, rhymed verse, and her mother. Wanton and faithless, she was given to regrettable pleasures with post-

impressionist poets, Bloomsbury intellectuals, and athletic Americans. That was what I heard, and no doubt it was true.[30]

Amongst previous manifestations of the "older woman" scenario of which Coward might have been thinking, the list includes Oscar Wilde's *Lady Windermere's Fan* (1892; filmed by Fred Paul in 1916 and Ernst Lubitsch in 1925); George Bernard Shaw's *Mrs. Warren's Profession* (1894); Arthur Wing Pinero's "Interesting Play" (as Hilaire Belloc appropriately quipped),[31] *The Second Mrs. Tanqueray* (1893, filmed by Fred Paul in 1916) and *The Notorious Mrs. Ebbsmith* (1895); Henry Arthur Jones's *Mrs. Dane's Defence* (1908); John Galsworthy's *The Skin Game* (1920, filmed by B.E. Doxattt-Pratt in 1921 and Hitchcock in 1931); William Somerset Maugham's *The Circle* (1921) and F.C. Burnand's lesser-known 1895 *Mrs. Ponderbury's Past* (revived 1907). I shall also draw upon *The Little Ottleys* (1908, 1912, 1916), a trio of novels by Wilde's friend and defender, Ada Leverson, and Elinor Glyn's infamous *Three Weeks* (1907), of which a film version, exploiting the supposed origins of the novel's heroine, was underway in Russia on the eve of Revolution. Coward may also have had in mind Gustave Flaubert's *Madame Bovary* (1856) and Collette's novel *Chéri* (1920), set in Paris and Neuilly in 1912.

However, the protagonists of this cycle of plays and novels do not necessarily constitute a coherent "set." Before *Cavalcade*, Coward is more interested in older women who have been misunderstood and socially condemned or ostracized for their pasts than older women who are aggressively vampish, although these, too, are present in British silent cinema (e.g., an actress with an exonerating, abusive past in *The Lure of Crooning Water* [dir. Arthur Rooke, 1920]). These are women who initiate encounters with ingenuous men. Contrary to Eric de Kuyper's assertion that women in British silent cinema appear to have nothing to do, these are women who actively "do."[32]

The falsely accused Larita in *Easy Virtue* may be contrasted with women who are explicitly cast as predators.

In *A Woman Redeemed* (dir. Sinclair Hill, 1927), the young wife of a member of a confederacy of foreign spies is ordered, against her will, to "vamp" a young English pilot (Brian Aherne) with whom she duly falls in love. In *Land of Hope and Glory* (dir. Harley Knowles, 1927), a Russian spy, Myra Almazov (Ruby Miller), seduces a young Ben Whiteford (Robin Irvine again in the role of a "boy") in order to obtain the secret plans for a new aircraft engine. Perhaps with this commonplace stereotype in mind, in the film of *Easy Virtue*, John's sisters (Dacita Deane and Dorothy Boyd) are surprised that Larita is not "dark and foreign looking."

Other experienced or older women prove their worth by refusing the attentions of younger suitors, by acknowledging that their attentions, however flattering, must be sacrificed in the interests of others. For instance, the cabaret dancer, Parysia, played by the alleged spy Olga Chekhova in E.A Dupont's *Moulin Rouge* (1928), declines Andre in favor of her own daughter, while proving equally attractive to Andre's father; in Dupont's *Piccadilly* (1929), Mabel (Gilda Gray) is made anxious by the arrival on the scene of a younger, more exotic rival, Shosho (Anna May Wong), for the attention of her fiancé, the cabaret impresario Valentine Wilmot (Jameson Thomas), whom she she resolves to hold onto. There are numerous other examples: Eugenia Raymond, in Leverson's novel *Love's Shadow* (1908), refuses Cecil—an absurd boy (ten years her junior), encouraging his marriage to Hyacinth Verney, and marries Cecil's uncle, Lord Selsey, while Bruce Ottley, in Leverson's *Love at Second Sight* (1916), proves his weakness by eloping with dominatrix Madame Frabelle, some twelve years his senior.[33] Frabelle is, in turn, the descendant of adventuresses in Victorian melodrama: for instance, the deliciously wicked Lydia Gwilt in Wilkie Collins's *Armadale* (1866), who at the instigation of her accomplice, the avaricious Mrs. Oldershaw, preys upon the affections of an unwitting scion of an extensive Norfolk estate. In Hitchcock's *Easy Virtue*, Larita defends herself in court against insinuations that she succumbed to the wealthy painter's proposals to rid herself of her odious marriage to an older man and finally admits her marriage to John as "cowardly." John, on his part, deems it a "mistake" — his mother has made him see it thus. John clearly proves himself the weaker vessel in his failure to honor his promise that "I love you, that's all that matters." Larita offers John a divorce in spite of the increased attention and opprobrium it will force upon her.

The character of John has both numerous precursors in fiction and also presages the role of the son in future mother-woman-son triangles in Hitchcock (notably, again, *Notorious*). Leverson, and Somerset Maugham in his short story "The Facts of Life," offer an explanation for the particular susceptibility of young boys to the charms of older women: the exclusively male environment of English public schools (as per *Downhill*) and university colleges provide little schooling for Life.[34] *Young Woodley* (dir. Thomas Bentley, 1928), an adaptation from John van Druten's much-discussed stage play, presents a sensitive and swayable schoolboy (Robin Irvine, yet again in such a role) falling for the disillusioned young wife (Marjorie Hume) of a dry and authoritative headmaster. Their shared love of poetry brings them together, but at the end, just as he is torn from her, she mournfully and dejectedly tears up his poems. Robin Woodley's father is evidently more a man of the world (like Colonel Whittaker in *Easy Virtue*) than the crusty husband: escorting his son home after the boy's expulsion, he urges him to consider the affair "an experience, not a tragedy." In her novel *The Edwardians* (1930), Vita Sackville-West commented somewhat archly that "For a young man to start his career with a love affair with an older woman was quite *de rigueur*" — Lucy (friend of Sylvia and mother to this "patrician adolescent") "had no cause to be uneasy, though she might perhaps have felt a tremor had she known how very passionately Sylvia had fallen in love with Sebastian."[35] The 1927 stage version of Noël Pemberton Billing's *High Treason* has the reprobate son of a curate falling prey to a manipulative, and older, married woman.[36] *Too Weak*, a 1907 spoof purportedly written by Ellova Gryn, lampoons callow youth confronted by the wiles of age, experience, and foreignness. In the original novel, Paul's father, Sir Charles

Figure 7

Verdayne, dispatches his valet to monitor proceedings. An affair (i.e., sowing one's oats) is one thing—an unsuitable attachment quite another:

> Saul dressed for dinner. I mention this to shew you what a nice clean person he really was. If I hadn't mentioned it you might have thought that he was one of those people who think the chief charm of being abroad is to shave every three days and to make a grey Jaeger shirt last a fortnight.[37]

Meanwhile, Olga Chekhova and, more especially, Mary Clare as Chloe Hornblower in Doxatt-Pratt's film of Galsworthy's *The Skin Game* (1920), are of a particular physical type, *une femme superbe*, as opposed to the 1920s cosmopolitan "tubular girl" or the home-grown product caricatured by Stevie Smith: "This Englishwoman is so refined / She has no bosom and no behind."[38] In the film of *Easy Virtue* lithe Larita has her maid cut down the back of her already low-cut dress, making a bracelet from the scraps, before her triumphant entry to the Moat House party (fig. 7). Hitchcock and his

Figure 8

editor intercut Larita's trumping preparations with the
welcoming of more substantially covered, amply bodied
guests, below. On stage, Cowl was "outrageously dressed
at a country gathering" and unsuitably bedazzling in
jewels: "the invading emeralds" had "without doubt strayed
into a country that knew not [Galsworthy's] Forsytes."[39] In
denial and defiance of Mrs. Whittaker's excusing claim that
Larita has "one of her headaches," Larita provocatively
attracts attention by making a spectacle of herself. She
determinedly exploits, to her own purposes, the image in
which she has been cast: "This is how his family always
pictured me," she confides to her former husband's
barrister, picking a stray feather from his sleeve. The
maid packs a trunk, already anticipating her mistress's
departure (Larita has determined her own destiny).
Larita assertively attempts to rouse John into action by
pausing, in her descent of the staircase, to tickle and tease
him with her huge ostrich fan (as per Cowl—a "Christmas
tree" on stage—"no wonder the decorous guests stare").[40]
(fig. 8) In further confirmation of her modernity, Larita
also smokes. A lot.

Sourcing and Contextualizing Easy Virtue: *The Moral?*

Sometimes mature vamps meet their match, only to be rejected. For instance, in Cutts's *Rat* series (*The Rat*, 1925; *The Triumph of the Rat*, 1926; *The Return of the Rat*, 1929), Zélie de Chaumet (Isabel Jeans) seduces Ivor Novello for her own amusement: "Had she been a man she would have been a Receiving Officer—as it was she took all she could get and asked for more," declares an intertitle before the Rat returns to an ever faithful child-woman sweetheart. Maurice Elvey's *The Woman Tempted* (released June 1926) transposes the action of Vera, countess of Cathcart's novel (a sort of Rhodesian *White Mischief*, opening with Elinor Glyn-style leopard-skin rugs), to a cavern in Cairo and a series of London drawing rooms and gardens. Louise Harding, persuasively portrayed by Juliette Compton, is, we are told, "married—monied—seeking in the Golden East the romance matrimony has denied her" at home. Louise intrigues Jimmy Duvivier (Warwick Ward). The cool and worldly Jimmy in turn impresses Louise, who is soon widowed. Louise proceeds to lavish her unshared inheritance on luxuriously revealing frocks and showy baubles: the film shows her poring over fashion magazines and matronly disapproval of her indecorous appearance. She is portrayed as Larita, in *Easy Virtue*, supposes herself to be perceived. Louise rejects a proposal from her current lover as "absurd"—she has no intention of remarrying— and he, being nothing but a "silly boy," duly throws himself under a tube train.[41] Jimmy eventually opts for a more conventional and conservative coupling with the younger but reassuringly much plainer Sybil (Joan Morgan)—ever the tediously obedient daughter.

Coward was avowedly, in his "modern" twist, modeling *Easy Virtue* on *fin de siècle* precedents, in his portrayal of a woman resisting oppression by whatever means necessary. In his apology for his "unpleasant play," *Mrs. Warren's Profession*, Shaw referred to its censorship by the Lord Chamberlain's Examiner of Plays and its denunciation by

certain critics and the press. Mrs. Warren, it should be
noted, refuses to apologize for her pragmatic decision to
escape poverty by becoming a prostitute in preference to
working in a white lead factory or throwing herself into the
chilly waters of the Thames. Shaw complained of
uncensored plays which end with "beautiful, exquisitely
dressed and sumptuously lodged and fed heroines," "dying
of consumption to the sympathetic tears of the whole
audience" or stepping "into the next room to commit
suicide, or at least to be turned out by their protectors and
passed on to be 'redeemed' by old and faithful lovers who
have adored them in spite of all their levities."[42] Such
"suicides" include Chloe in *The Skin Game*, Paula Tanqueray,
Iris Storm, Hermina Burton in Grant Allen's phenomenally
popular (but ultimately conservative) *The Woman Who Did*
(1895, reverently filmed by Walter West in 1915) and
Agnes's self-mortification in Pinero's *The Notorious Mrs.
Ebbsmith*. Louise, in *The Woman Tempted*, comes to a sticky
end. Such "redemptions" include Mrs. Erlynne (finally,
Isabel Jeans's favorite role) in *Lady Windermere's Fan*.[43] In
Pinero's *Iris* (filmed by Cecil Hepworth in 1915 from the
original 1901 stageplay, revived in 1925 at the Adelphi, with
Coward's friend and frequent co-star, Gladys Cooper, in the
title role and Ivor Novello as Laurence Trenwith), the
marriage of a wealthy widow to her impoverished boyish
lover is impeded by society's expectation that a husband
should provide for a wife in the manner to which she has
become accustomed. A "redemption" — marriage to a
millionaire financier — has catastrophic consequences.[44]
Pinero's *His House in Order* (1905) was directed on film by
the actor Randle Ayrton in 1928 with a smoldering Tallulah
Bankhead as Nina, the second Mrs. Filmer Jesson.[45] For
Bankhead, reputedly receiving the highest salary yet paid to
the star of a British film — and who, as a Bright Young
Person incarnate, provided as much indirect, objective
offstage copy as Jeans delivered directly, subjectively, as
supposed author of her offstage articles — this was a typical
"negligée" role, with "an inevitable bedroom scene," akin to

Larita's bedroom scenes in Nice and Norfolk in *Easy Virtue*.[46] In *His House in Order* it is the first, deceased Mrs. Jesson who is discovered—predictably by a stash of hidden letters—not to be the saintly paragon of virtue she has been hitherto held to be, to the detriment of her successor, and, as in Leverson, she compassionately, sensitively declines and deflects the attentions of a younger admirer. Shaw, on the other hand, boldly presents a heroine who recognizes no need for atonement or self-sacrifice. The privileged education of Mrs. Warren's daughter, the likewise pragmatic but exemplary New Woman, Vivie, has been paid for from the proceeds of her mother's profession. Once made aware of the source of her maintenance, Vivie determines to support herself. Mrs. Warren is, undoubtedly, a "woman with a past," like Larita in *Easy Virtue*. For Shaw, who refuses to repudiate his heroine, the "moral" problem becomes the prospect of a marriage between Vivie and her half brother, the suspected outcome of an erstwhile liaison between his clergyman father (sewing his own seed) and the young Kitty Warren.

Whatever its moral and social implications, one of the dramatic virtues of Shaw's play is that Mrs. Warren's past is revealed successively, during the course of the action. Eliot Stannard's adaptation of Coward for Hitchcock's *Easy Virtue* typically reveals Larita's past at the outset, tidily book-ending the scenario with a pair of courtroom scenes—the same ancient, myopic judge presiding over a court first crowded, ultimately deserted.[47] We are shown Larita's past in a lengthy flashback sequence, thereby denying it any sense of mystery or expectation—all we can do is wait for the Whittakers to discover it for themselves (Hitchcockian suspense, rather than surprise). In his adaptation Stannard correspondingly retains key locations, scenes, and character attributes while dispersing and redistributing crucial fragments of Coward's dialogue.[48] Not only does Larita flee England to forget unwelcome "Reporters—Photographers—Publicity" "on the tolerant shores of the Mediterranean," but it is also John's father, Colonel Whittaker (Frank Elliot)—Coward suggests that he has a history of "levities" himself—who acknowledges that she is "a very fascinating woman, my boy," while his wife frostily greets her with "I trust that you won't be bored by our simple family life."[49]

The coupling of John and Larita has precedents in the plays to which Coward consciously offered *Easy Virtue* in homage, and has parallels in the novels of Coward's key contemporaries. In *Easy Virtue*, Larita first encounters John, an athletic healthy type in flannels, on a tennis court. He inadvertently hits a ball in her eye. John is a match for Tom Veryan in Coward's *The Vortex* (1924), adapted by Stannard and directed by Adrian Brunel (released September 1927). Larita, the "older" woman, as in *The Woman Tempted*, ousts a presumed, local intended, Sarah (Enid Stamp-Taylor). Mrs. Whittaker cruelly seats Sarah between the newlyweds at dinner, and John and Larita talk across her. In the absence of Larita, John and Sarah have nothing to say to one another. Yet Sarah, the "peacemaker," who Larita eventually admits "should have married" John, is selflessly magnanimous in her pity of the couple's plight—"I'm terribly sorry for both of them"—thus proving her worth. Similarly, Venice, Napier's wife, cedes place to Iris in Arlen's *The Green Hat*:

> I'd stuff all the marriage-laws down a drain-pipe rather than keep them apart for another minute. And I think you must be mad and bad not to see the loveliness of a love like Iris's—and after all this time she's beaten you all in the end, and I'm glad, so glad, so glad![50]

Perhaps Sarah admires Larita's bravery. In Coward's *Easy Virtue*, she says to John that he has taken his opportunity and "married for love," and she respects him for it: "If we'd married, it would have been for friendship and convenience," a disadvantage in married life.[51] Pity is here, as Shakespeare once suggested, "a grize towards love," as opposed to a cynical jury woman's suspicion that Larita's pity for the painter's devotion is akin to love—subsequently persuaded by the barrister's oratory to amend and add "nearly 2000 a year" to her scribbled notes.[52] As in *The Skin Game*, one of John's sisters supports the "older" woman. Hilda, in *Easy Virtue*, is more supportive than brogued, tweedy, and priggish Marion, and thinks it fun to have Larita as sister-in-law. Hilda may well wish to follow Larita's example and rid herself of the shackles of her conventional home life. Certainly, she is more spontaneously excited than affronted at the sight of Larita in the pages of the *Tatler*. Stannard having excised Coward's secondary characters (the admiring Charles Burleigh and the adoring puppyish Philip Borden), Sarah, outside of the family, is left alone to shoulder the burden of support for Larita.

Sympathy for the "older" woman in *Easy Virtue* is comparable to the apportioning of support in the texts on which Coward was drawing. Jean Chothia has observed that after the turn of the century, the "woman with a past" theme surfaced "in distinguishing the attitude and assumptions of the protagonists from the more conservative older generation."[53] Such a difference is exemplified in, for instance, Henry Arthur Porter's *Mrs. Dane's Defence* (1900), by the contrast of the suburban matriarch, Mrs. Bulsom-Porter (mirrored by Mrs. Whittaker) and the ironic yet more sympathetic and younger Lady Eastney (something of a parallel to Coward's Sarah). In *Easy Virtue* there is also a striking difference between Colonel Whittaker, who manfully defends Larita—her "past life is no affair of ours"—and Mrs. Whittaker, who replies that "On the contrary, it will utterly disgrace us—it will make us the gossip of the entire countryside!" Colonel Whittaker attempts to soothe his daughter-in-law: "It will all come right, Larita—if my boy still loves you." In Pinero's *The Notorious Mrs. Ebbsmith*, set in Venice, the worldly, not to say rakish, Duke of St. Olpherts, admires Mrs. Ebbsmith for her independence, never having been able to approach women "in a missionary spirit."[54] By way of contrast, his nephew, an ambitious Coming Man, concerned by the shadow such an attachment may cast on his own public image, seeks to make a "conventional" rather than a "companionable" wife of her. In *His House in Order*, it is

Filmer Jesson's brother, Hilary, older in years but younger in spirit—and significantly a well-travelled man—who supports Nina. In other words, "modernity" cannot be presumed to be the prerogative of younger characters. However, in the literature of the time, it is as frequently suggested that there is something peculiarly stifling in English social mores (as in Hitchcock's *Rich and Strange* [1932]) as it is that another generation is more enlightened. In *Mrs. Warren's Profession*, Kitty Warren has been living abroad with Mr. Crofts, running hotels (i.e., keeping brothels). In 1926, *The Sketch*, apropos of Paula Tanqueray, acknowledging Coward's sourcing, reworking, and his modern "twist," commented that "It was the woman who was 'wrong'"—as in the divine Iris in *Iris*— "and not the country, whereas Mr. Coward would have it the other way about."[55]

The Gigolo

In contemporaneous couplings of the "older" woman and the younger man, the former is not necessarily a divorcee (as in *Easy Virtue*) or a widow. She may equally be the bored wife of an inattentive husband. These women fall prey to, or themselves prey upon, a concomitant 1920s type: the gigolo. This figure was to be found in the pages of the popular press as often as he appeared in popular fiction, often sharing with *Easy Virtue* and Hitchcock's *To Catch a Thief* (1955) a Continental setting. John, in *Easy Virtue*, is not a gigolo, just as Larita (as both Coward and Hitchcock demonstrate) is not an adventuress, but there lurks a danger of misapprehension, explicitly for Larita and, perhaps, implicitly for John, circumstantially infected by the aura of the gigolo.

According to the *Oxford English Dictionary*, the *Woman's Home Companion* in 1922 commented that "a gigolo, generally speaking, is a man who lives off women's money . . . one of those incredible and pathetic male creatures . . . who for ten francs . . . would dance with any woman wishing to dance in the cafés, hotels and restaurants of France." The *Daily News* added, in 1927, that gigolos may otherwise be known as "lounge lizards."[56] In *Six Days* (1924), Elinor Glyn describes David Lamont, with his olive skin and jet-black hair brushed back from his brow, gleaming "like a silk hat," looking like a gigolo, while David himself jealously refers to one of Laline Lester's former admirers as "just a tango partner."[57] In *Paradise* (dir. Denison Clift, 1928), the stout Lady Liverage (Barbara Gott) is affronted and jealous when her usual partner, Spiridoff (Alexander d'Arcy) prefers the company of a girl, Kitty Cranson (Betty Balfour), who is spending the prize money from a crossword competition on a dream trip to the Riviera: "I'll never, never dance again with that sleek-haired lounge lizard!," Lady Liverage insists. Dr. John Halliday (Joseph Striker) duly arrives at the hotel to escort the girl safely back to England and her father's vicarage: "That gigolo is unworthy of you . . . of your father's good name" and the Riviera is cast as a "dangerous playground." To be sure of her return, Halliday purloins the girl's remaining cash.

Gigolos in film and literature are usually foreign or at least foreign-looking. Rudolph Valentino is, of course, the embodiment of the type. In Rex Ingram's *The Four Horsemen of the Apocalypse* (1921), the Italian-born actor plays an Argentinean who, as the film opens, is passing his time as a tango partner; by the end of the film, his enlistment and war service have redeemed him. In *Downhill*, the descent of an exemplary English public schoolboy is marked by his partnering elderly and washed-up women in dance halls in Marseilles. A horrifying "Poetess" (Violet Farebrother), old enough to be his mother, propositions him "in the cold light of day." Irène Némirovsky's *David Golder* (set in Biarritz in 1926) and *Paradise* cast supposedly aristocratic Russian emigrés as dance partners—akin to the "phony" Prince Ivan in Hitchcock's *The Pleasure Garden* (1925): a dog can sniff a rat and duly barks at him.[58] The superlatively sleek Spiridoff tells Kitty that he is an exile "and a dancing monkey to rich old women." In Geza von Bolvary's *Champagner* (1929), a waiter (Jack Trevor) is seduced into the role of gigolo by the wife of a richer and older man.

Similar settings (e.g., the Riviera) and character types recur elsewhere. In *Confetti*, set in Nice, there is, again, an older woman and a "boy". In "Gigolo and Gigolette," set in locations with which Somerset Maugham in the 1920s was personally familiar, Paco Espinel is the real thing, an Argentinean employed to express admiration of the "opulent, aging charms" of the casino's female clientele—and to urge them to gamble or "to dance with stout women who wanted to get their weight down."[59] For Cockney Syd, however, it is an inescapably sad misfortune that he looks the part:

> Syd had been a dancing gigolo since he was eighteen, he was very good-looking in his dark Spanish way and full of life, old women and middle-aged women were glad to pay to dance with him . . . . He had drifted from England to the Continent and there he had stayed, going from hotel to hotel, to the Riviera in the winter, to watering places in France in the summer. Sometimes a middle-aged woman would ask one to spend a night with her, and he would get two hundred and fifty francs for that. There was always the chance of a silly old fool losing her head. . . . One of Syd's friends had married one of them, who was old enough to be his mother, but she gave him a car and money to gamble with, and they lived in a beautiful villa at Biarritz.[60]

Roddy is deemed "very cheap at fifty francs a dance," in *Downhill*, while Julia's accomplice in Roddy's seduction appears happy to live off Julia's money (by way of Julia's marriage to Roddy Berwick). In Coward's *Cavalcade*, a white-haired mother who has lost her sons in war is set against her "brassy" friend who dances with a boy of an age to be her own son.[61] While Mrs. Whittaker, in *Easy Virtue*, presumes that Larita, the "older" woman, is an adventuress, there is also the possibility that the "boy" be cast correspondingly, demeaningly, as a gigolo in their coupling. The gigolo is despised for his "unmanly" means of earning a living (as opposed to the "manly" sacrifice, required even of boys) and for his overt, "unmanly" display of his charms. As Mary Ann Doane has remarked, the male striptease and the gigolo inevitably signify a mechanism of reversal, "constituting themselves as aberrations."[62] The feminization of the brilliantined, thin-moustached "lounge lizard," Juan José — who poses as the Count Lorenz Alban for the purposes of his affair with the older Lady King (Hilda Moore), in Maurice Elvey's 1928 *Palais de Danse* (with its intertitle references to Coward) — is rendered clearly in John Longden's performance — he habitually preens and polishes his nails.[63] Novello, as Roddy, is presented, in point of view, discomforted in his semi-nakedness by Tim's sister — he grasps for a towel — then objectified again, upside-down, in Julia's view to her dressing room doorway, then, again, on the dance floor, in *Downhill*.

Conclusion

While both Arlen's *The Green Hat* and *Easy Virtue* appear to offer a modern twist on old shapes, neither differs from "older" woman precursors in that they still require a gesture of "feminine" sacrifice for the resolution of their narratives (Iris Storm's suicide; Larita's departure for offstage Paris — the Ritz "next room" — in Coward and, in Hitchcock, we know not where on her exit from the court.) As in Coward, implicitly, the second divorce is left undefended. Coward has Sarah wishing Larita the best for her future while Hitchcock has Sarah and Larita exchanging a final kiss — a blessing on her valued friendship, against the odds — and a wish for her soulmate's future, with or without John.

Stannard's structural reorganization of the narrative of *Easy Virtue* prioritizes legal process and social propriety (as do Coward's precedents, *Mrs. Dane's Defence* and *Iris*). This reframing might be read as a sardonic critique, leaving personal compassion, understanding, and broadmindedness, as exemplified by Colonel Whittaker and Sarah, as the Coward "core" to Hitchcock's film. Coward is critical of provincial middle-class hypocrisy, as vocalized, with appropriate laconic urbanity, by Larita. More is lost in the film than Coward's repartee: there is a diminution of Larita's agency. However, by way of compensation, Hitchcock widens the scope of a domestic drama (a comedy of manners), narratively, geographically and socially, condemning a public appetite for gossip and scandal in which, by way of direct address, the audience becomes complicit. Hitchcock's Larita is explicitly wronged as the victim of salacious media attention. In the film the *declassé* Larita is made afraid of the notoriety that the discovery of her misunderstood past will heap upon her, and of the threat that this presents to her new-found happiness with John, who fails to stand by her when it is exposed. Hitchcock ultimately delivers a more vulnerable, disempowered Larita than does Coward. Conversely, the fact that Sybil, in *The Woman Tempted*, is "suitably" married-off to an older man "with a past" passes without question. The "older man" scenario is sufficiently commonplace to be unremarkable. Different rules continue to be applied to the conduct of men and women and an old double standard is retained intact—even reinforced—by the experience of the war. Hitchcock's twist on Coward's *Easy Virtue* reflects on the plight—and the pity—of both the younger man and the older woman confronted by conservative public scrutiny, ever eager to condemn. In Hitchcock's *Easy Virtue*, Larita's reputation—her unjustly presumed guilt—not only literally precedes her but is also a burden thrust upon her from which she is finally unable to escape.

Notes

With thanks to Twentieth Century Flicks, Bristol, as ever, and to Sid Gottlieb, as previously, for astute and patient commentary on drafts of this article.

1. Sarah to Charles in Noël Coward, *Easy Virtue* (1924), in *Play Parade* vol. II (London: William Heinemann, 1950), Act III.
2. In *The Lodger* (1926), for instance, the sensational news of the Avenger and his Tuesday night victims is simultaneously carried

across telegraph, newspapers, and radio. See John Bruns, "Hitchcock's Newspaper: A 'Thing in the Crowd' " *Hitchcock Annual* 18 (2013): 72-106.

3. University of Bristol Theatre Collection, MM 1127: *The Sketch*, 1 April 1925, xxxix (and 1927 "Beauty Supplement") and *Daily News* articles on fashion: "Wise skirts: short but not too short"; *The Queen*, 12 October 1927, "Isabel Jeans in a gown of silver tissue with fringe and beaded embroidery worn in *Easy Virtue*." See also accompanying souvenir cigarette cards. The star status of Jeans is indicated by capitalizing her name in the credits introducing *Downhill* and her above-the-title credit for *Easy Virtue*.

4. See Thomas Leitch, *Find the Director and Other Hitchcock Games* (Athens, Georgia: University of Georgia Press, 1991), 53.

5. "Healthy types in flannels" were already considered something of a Coward cliché, hence the citation in the film version of *Easy Virtue*.

6. James M. Vest, in "Recurrent Visual Patterns in *Downhill*," *Hitchcock Annual* 15 (2006-2007), 38-84, echoing Maurice Yacowar, *Hitchcock's British Films* (Hamden, Conn.: Archon Books, 1977), 49, comments that Roddy is "framed to seem a boy in a man's world"(65), but in this scene, interrogated by the headmaster, Roddy performs and conducts himself in a more manly fashion than Tim.

7. In Coward's version, Larita smashes a smirking statuette of the Venus de Milo.

8. Michael Williams, "'Cocktails,' 'Post-War Hysteria' and 'Decadence': Noël Coward and British Silent Cinema," in Alan Burton and Laraine Porter, eds., *Scene-Stealing* (Flicks Books: Trowbridge, 2003), 102-09, at 105.

9. Patrick McGilligan, *Alfred Hitchcock: A Life in Darkness and Light* (New York: Regan Books, 2003), reports Hitchcock's observation that this was the worst title to which he ever laid claim, ensuring "that it wouldn't be forgotten" (92). See also, William K. Everson, "Rediscovery," *Films in Review*, 26, no. 5 (May 1975): 293-99, at 296.

10. Tom Ryall, *Alfred Hitchcock and the British Cinema* (1986; London: Athlone, 1996), 117, citing Ivor Montagu.

11. As Thomas Leitch, in "*Notorious*: Hitchcock's Pivotal Film," *Hitchcock Annual* 17 (2011), astutely remarks, such moments of levity and shifts of tone "express not merely an alternation between grave and gay but an emphasis on melodrama as uncanny and surreal by contrasting moments of emotional intensity with the rhythms of everyday life" (19).

28 Amy Sargeant

12. Lesley Brill, *The Hitchcock Romance: Love and Irony in Hitchcock's Films* (Princeton: Princeton University, 1988), 93.
13. Leitch, "*Notorious*," 34-35; Brill, *The Hitchcock Romance*, 89, 109.
14. Coward, *Easy Virtue*, Act I.
15. Steve Jacobs, *The Wrong House: The Architecture of Alfred Hitchcock* (Rotterdam: 010 Publishers, 2007), 163-64; see also Leitch, *Find the Director*, 53.
16. Langley Court in Liss, Hampshire, for the exterior of *Easy Virtue*'s Moat House; the frieze is, perhaps, a vestige of the religiosity of Mrs. Whittaker and married daughter Marion in Coward's play.
17. John Rylands Library, Manchester, Basil Dean Archive, DEA/2/19/2; for further discussion of *The Queen Was in the Parlour*, see Amy Sargeant, "Ruritanian Romps: Kitsch Sentiment and Style," *LISA e-journal*, forthcoming.
18. James Agate review, *Sunday Times*, 13 June 1926, MM/REF/PE/UR/CNO/15/13. Stephen Elliott's 2008 remake of *Easy Virtue* casts an American (Jessica Biel) as Larita and makes more of nationality and of her urban origins (versus the countrified Whittakers) than age as a "disqualifying" difference. John's father (Colin Firth), a war veteran, has been to Paris and, as in the Coward and Hitchcock versions, is supportive of Larita. The soundtrack refers to Cole Porter ("Mad About the Boy," its lyrics referring to a gigolo) and to Coward ("Mad Dogs and Englishmen"). Larita here suffers from hay fever and the call is raised: "Anyone for tennis?"
19. MM/REF/PE/UR/CNO/15/23/1: in April 1927, in Westcliff-on-Sea; in May, in Swansea; in August, in Brighton.
20. MM 1127 re. *Beauty* at the Strand: "Miss Jeans vamped nineteen to the resplendent dozen."
21. Christine Gledhill, *Reframing British Cinema 1918-1928: Between Restraint and Passion* (London: BFI, 2003), 113, citing the *Evening Standard*, 21 August 1926.
22. MM/REF/PE/UR/CNO/15/13.
23. Michael Balcon, in *Michael Balcon Presents . . . A Lifetime in Film* (London: Hutchinson, 1969), recalls that, while Coward was obviously wildly fashionable and widely talented, the silent film versions of Coward's *The Vortex* and *Easy Virtue* were commercial failures: "the plays were deprived of their very essence, the words!" (27).
24. Eric Rohmer and Claude Chabrol, trans. Stanley Hochman, *Hitchcock: The First Forty-Four Films* (New York: Frederick Ungar, 1979), 12. Raymond Durgnat is similarly dismissive of Hitchcock's "last film with Gainsborough," in *The Strange Case of Alfred Hitchcock*

(London: Faber & Faber, 1974), 77, while Robin Wood finds Larita a "not very" interesting precursor of Hitchcock's future "guilty" women in *Hitchcock's Films Revisited* (New York: Columbia University Press, 2002), 242; see also Leitch, *Find the Director*, 53-54.

25. Coward, in *Autobiography* (1937; London: Mandarin, 1992), 158.

26. Coward, *Play Parade*, ix.

27. Coward, *Cavalcade* (London: William Heinemann, 1932), Part III, Scene 2, set in 1930.

28. See Diana Souhami, *Mrs. Keppel and Her Daughter* (London: Harper Collins, 1996).

29. Dikran Kouyoumdjian [Michael Arlen], *The Green Hat: A Romance for a Few People* (1924; London: Cassell, 1968), 113. Coward provided the introduction to Arlen's *The London Venture* (1920; London: Cassell, 1968), ix, commenting that Arlen lent funds for the 1924 London production of Coward's *The Vortex*, with Coward starring as Nicky Lancaster, which transferred to New York and played alongside Arlen's *The Green Hat* in September 1925. Coward noted that *The Vortex* "was enthusiastically hailed by the critics and established me as the most promising playwright of the decade" (Coward, *Autobiography*, 150). See also Amy Sargeant, *British Cinema: A Critical History* (London: BFI, 2005), 95.

30. Michael Arlen, "Confessions of a Naturalised Englishman," in *The Short Stories of Michael Arlen* (London: W. Collins Sons & Co. Ltd., n.d.), 7, 35-36. Arlen could have—backhandedly—returned a compliment: in the same volume, in "Portrait of a Lady on Park Avenue," he introduces Consuelo as emotionally unimportant, "like a play by Mr. Noël Coward, but her construction was faultless, like a play by Mr. Noël Coward."

31. Hilaire Belloc, "Matilda, Who Told Lies, and Was Burned to Death," in *Cautionary Verses* (London: Duckworth, 1985), 17-24, 21-22.

32. Eric de Kuyper made this comment regarding the insipidity of women in British silent cinema in an invited paper given at the Nottingham British Silent Film Festival 2005, but is not alone in this misapprehension. See also Kenton Bamford, *Distorted Images: British National Identity and Film in the 1920s* (London: I.B. Tauris, 1999), 34-35, 98.

33. Ada Leverson, *The Little Ottleys* (London: MacGibbon & Kee, 1962). In *His House in Order*, the heroine similarly deflects the unsought-for attentions of a younger admirer; see Coward, *Play Parade*, ix.

34. Leverson, *Love's Shadow* (1908), in *The Little Ottleys*, 205; William Somerset Maugham, "The Facts of Life," in *The World Over: The Collected Stories* (London: The Reprint Society, 1954), 813-29, at 815, first published in 1951 but written decades earlier, in which eighteen-year old Nicky has what is deemed by his fathers' friends to be a "lucky" escape from an "adventuress" encountered during a three-day tennis tournament in Monte Carlo.

35. Vita Sackville-West, *The Edwardians* (1930; London: Virago, 1983), 99-100. In Coward's *Easy Virtue*, Act II, Larita acerbically remarks to Mrs. Whittaker: "I suppose you wouldn't consider it betraying his honour if he'd had an affair with me and not married me?"

36. See Amy Sargeant, "Scientific Marvels and Sartorial Surprises: Maurice Elvey's *High Treason* (1929)," *Journal of British Cinema and Television* 4, no. 1 (2007): 37-50; also *Theatre and Film Illustrated*, MM/REF/TH/LO/Strand.

37. Ellova Gryn, *Too Weak* (London: Craddock & Co., 1907), 21.

38. See Aldous Huxley, *Chrome Yellow* (1921; Frogmore: Triad Panther, 1977), 85, and Stevie Smith, "This Englishwoman," in *Selected Poems* (London: Penguin, 2002), 48.

39. MM/REF/PE/UR/CNO/15/13.

40. MM/REF/PE/UR/CNO/15/13.

41. Vera, Countess of Cathcart, *The Woman Tempted* (London: John Lang, 1926).

42. George Bernard Shaw, *The Bodley Head George Bernard Shaw: Collected Plays with Their Prefaces*, vol. I (London: Bodley Head, 1970), 237. There is no film version of *Mrs. Warren's Profession*, which was privately performed in 1902 but banned from the public stage until 1925.

43. Ian Herbert, ed., *Who's Who in the Theatre* (London: Pitman, 1978), 778-79.

44. MM/REF/TH/LO/ADE/23. A critic commented of a play originally considered "daring" that "modern audiences wonder why poor for Iris's tragedy should have so shocked."

45. MM/REF/TH/LO/LYR/32. Bankhead drew extraordinary applause from "Girls in the Gallery," appearing also on stage in 1925 in Coward's *Fallen Angels*.

46. *Daily Telegraph* 13 December 1968, newspaper clipping, MM/REF/TH/LO/ADE/23. See also, *Theatre and Film Illustrated*, December 1928, 1, reporting Bankhead's engagement to Count Anthony Basardi. Bankhead was an habituée of Soho's Bohemian Gargoyle Club; Kate Figes, *The Big Fat Bitch Book* (London: Virago,

2007), reports her as once saying: "I'll come to make love to you at five o'clock. If I'm late, start without me" (48).

47. Stannard similarly reconfigured J.M. Barrie's one-act play *The Twelve Pound Look* for Jack Denton's 1920 film, such that the final "revelation" on stage occurs at the beginning of the corresponding film.

48. Charles Barr, *English Hitchcock* (Moffat: Cameron & Hollis, 1999), claims that *Easy Virtue* "takes none of its dialogue titles from Coward"(118), but this isn't strictly true; dialogue is, rather, reattributed and paraphrased, retaining its original force and effect.

49. For the Mediterranean as location and thematic setting in British silent cinema, see Amy Sargeant, *"We're All Doing the Riviera* Because *It's So Much Nicer in Nice,"* in Laraine Porter and Bryony Dixon, eds., *Picture Perfect: Landscape, Place and Travel in British Cinema before 1930* (Exeter: Exeter Press, 2007), 92-103. Pinero's *The Second Mrs. Tanqueray* opens with a reference to a meeting on the Riviera.

50. Arlen, *The Green Hat*, 238.

51. Coward, *Easy Virtue*, Act II.

52. In Shakespeare's *Twelfth Night*, Act III, Scene 2, Viola says to Olivia, denying that pity is a grize [a step] to love: "No, not a grize; for 'tis a vulgar proof / That very oft we pity enemies" (ll. 124-25).

53. Jean Chothia, "Introduction," in *The New Woman and Other Emancipated Woman Plays* (Oxford: Oxford University Press, 1998), xiii.

54. Arthur Wing Pinero, *The Notorious Mrs. Ebbsmith*, Clayton Hamilton, ed., *The Social Plays of Arthur Wing Pinero* (New York: AMS Press, 1967), Act IV, Scene 1.

55. MM/REF/PE/UR/CNO/15/13: review, 13 June 1926.

56. *Oxford English Dictionary*, gigolo: citing *Woman's Home Companion*, 7 November 1922 and *Daily News*, 21 May 1927. Evidently, the word was still thought to have currency in 2007, with the release of Richard Bracewell's *The Gigolos*, with professional ladies' men servicing London's middle-aged middle-class.

57. Elinor Glyn, *Six Days* (1924; Bath: Lythway Press, 1968), 9, 153.

58. Irène Némirovsky, *David Golder* (1929; London: Vintage, 2007), 37-38.

59. Somerset Maugham, "Gigolo and Gigolette," in *The World Over*, 830-45, 831. For further examples of the effeminized gigolo in concurrent English literature, see John Buchan, *The Three Hostages* (1924), in *The Complete Richard Hannay* (London: Penguin, 2013), 825, 838; P.G. Wodehouse, *The Adventures of Sally* (1922; London: Arrow Books, 2008), 180; and George Orwell's memoir of the 1920s, *Down*

and Out in London and Paris (1933; Harmondsworth: Penguin, 1968), 60. For the achievement and extensive influence of the Argentinean tango, see Eric Hobsbawm, *Age of Extremes* (London: Michael Joseph, 1995), 197.

60. Maugham, "Gigolo and Gigolette," 841-42; see also, for comparable character types and setting, Agatha Christie, "The Soul of the Croupier," in *The Mysterious Mr. Quin* (1930; London: Harper Collins, 2003), 127-53.

61. Coward, *Cavalcade*, Part III, Scene 2.

62. Mary Ann Doane, *Femmes Fatales* (London: Routledge, 1991), 2; see also,for the systematic feminization of Valentino's persona as primary object of spectacle, Miriam Hansen, "Pleasure, Ambivalence, Identification: Valentino and Female Spectatorship," in Christine Gledhill, ed., *Stardom* (1991; London: Routledge, 2000), 259-82.

63. For further discussion of *Palais de Danse*, see Gledhill, *Reframing British Cinema*, 175-77, and Sargeant, *British Cinema*, 85.

HENRY K. MILLER

Sympathetic Guidance:
Hitchcock and C.A. Lejeune

The professional relationship of C.A. Lejeune and Alfred Hitchcock has a classic rise-and-fall structure. It began at the start of both their careers in the early 1920s, started to turn around the time of Hitchcock's move to Hollywood in 1939, and came to an unhappy end on the afternoon of Thursday 4 August 1960, at the Plaza Cinema on Lower Regent Street, during the London preview of *Psycho* (1960). " 'Who does he think he is!' Caroline Lejeune repeated, as we left, shaken and shocked," her fellow critic Alexander Walker would recall of this occasion, claiming that "she promptly handed in her resignation from the *Observer*. If that's the way films were going, she wanted none of it."[1] By her own account she had in fact left the screening before Walker, keeping the ending secret by default, "for the simple reason that I grew so sick and tired of the whole beastly business that I didn't stop to see it. Your edict may keep me out of the theatre, my dear Hitchcock," she wrote, referring to the famous ban on latecomers, "but I'm hanged if it will keep me in."[2] She filed her final review for the paper at the end of the year.

It was their last public disagreement, but not their first. An earlier occasion, Lejeune's response to *Sabotage* (1936), is part of Hitchcock lore, repeated in more than one interview. Hitchcock alluded to it when he recounted to Peter Bogdanovich that "The critics were very angry. One woman said, 'I could hit you.' "[3] In another version, given by the film's screenwriter Charles Bennett, at a party after the press screening "she came up to me and said, 'Charles, you should be ashamed of yourself for killing that child.' "[4]

These incidents, both apparently attesting to a critical sensibility shaped in an age very different from our own, have not helped improve a reputation which has been tainted more generally by a single, much-quoted column of September 1947. During a slow patch, more than a quarter-century after she began weekly reviewing, Lejeune came to reflect that most of what she had to see was "bosh," and after writing that "it is not easy for a critic to give up the pretence that the thing he is criticising is an art," did just that.[5] "I am ready to declare categorically that films are not an art," she wrote two weeks later, "and I feel very much the better for it."[6] The line was instantly seized upon by the young critics who had recently founded *Sequence* magazine, starting with Penelope Houston, who quoted it, appalled, in *Sequence*'s first "national" edition just a few weeks later, and then in her debut piece for *Sight and Sound* in 1949.[7] Fifteen years later, Houston, by then *Sight and Sound*'s editor, brought it up again in a review of Lejeune's autobiography which began with the double-edged statement: "Perhaps the most surprising thing about Caroline Lejeune, as these reminiscences reveal her, was her decision to become a film critic."[8]

But it was Lindsay Anderson's famous call to arms, "Stand Up! Stand Up!," published in the first issue of *Sight and Sound* that Houston edited, in the autumn of 1956, that did the most lasting damage. Surveying cinema's road to "respectability" over three decades, starting with the founding of the Film Society and the little magazine *Close Up* in the mid-1920s, Anderson saw a loss of "passion," even a loss of "seriousness," and argued that for all that cinema had been made respectable, "the significance of the cinema—or rather the acknowledgement of its significance—has actually been reduced."[9] As evidence he produced the "classic instance" of what amounted to a *trahison des clercs*: "Miss C.A. Lejeune's column in the *Observer* just nine years ago."

Lejeune, as one of the two "Sunday Ladies" (with Dilys Powell) who dominated British newspaper film criticism in the postwar era, stood for the establishment from which Houston and Anderson's generation naturally had to break; but she retained this position for a subsequent generation as well. Four years later, during the debate over auteurism in which *Sight and Sound* represented the *ancien régime*, in part because of its treatment of Hitchcock, Charles Barr, then an undergraduate writing in the Cambridge magazine *Granta*— its cover graced with a still of Norman Bates—was able to re-quote Lejeune's "notorious statement of September 14th, 1947," having unearthed Houston's *Sequence* review, and declared that Lejeune epitomized "the faults of British film journalism," faults from which *Sight and Sound*, with its "common-sense and unimaginative" outlook, was not immune.[10] Nor was her retirement, which came a few weeks after Barr's article appeared, the end of it. The same column, this time re-quoted from Anderson, did service again in 1972, when the *Movie* critic V.F. Perkins, on the very first page of his book *Film as Film*, wrote that "As late as 1947, the *Observer*'s film reviewer decided that films were nothing but 'bits of celluloid and wire,' and thus felt 'ready to declare categorically that films are not an art.' "[11]

Thus did Lejeune's reputation suffer in posterity, having united at least two otherwise opposed generations of British critics against her: generally as a naysayer towards cinema's claims to art status in the heroic age of auteurism, and specifically as a doubter of the auteurists' idol, Alfred Hitchcock—more particularly, of late Hitchcock.

Relaying and amplifying this consensus, the major work on Hitchcock's canonization since the 1950s, Robert Kapsis's *Hitchcock: The Making of a Reputation*, situates Lejeune, described as "England's premier critic," firmly on the wrong side of history, together with the old guard of New York reviewers, during "the transformation of Hitchcock's reputation from popular entertainer to serious auteur."[12] As Kapsis writes on his first page, stating his thesis, "Prior to the 1960s, most American film critics and scholars did not rank Hitchcock's films as 'serious art,' in large measure because in their view significant work could not be achieved in the 'thriller' genre."[13] In his account, the change came with the adoption by American critics of the precepts established by *Cahiers du Cinéma*, which "meant treating the films of 'favored' directors such as Hitchcock as the works of a single creative mind."[14] By contrast, according to Kapsis, "England's mainstream reviewers never really adopted the view of Hitchcock as a serious artist. Rather, they have continued to feel more comfortable with the Hitchcock who made those "entertaining 'little British comedy thrillers' back in the thirties."[15]

What is in question is not Lejeune's response to the later films, which was no doubt inadequate, but the stark yet insufficiently expounded dichotomy, structuring not only Kapsis's book but much of the discourse, popular and scholarly, on auteurism and Hitchcock, between "popular entertainer" and "serious artist." It is probably a postmodern bromide to say that these categories were never more than provisional, but Lejeune's full record shows it to be true.

Perhaps more importantly, it also reveals something about Hitchcock himself which the dichotomy tends to obscure: how Hitchcock became a serious artist, whether or not he was recognized as one. This question has not gone unaddressed, and the most compelling account is that given by Peter Wollen, according to whom Hitchcock "acquired his cultivated interest in modern art, his perfectionism, his willingness to experiment and his fascination with new techniques" from the organization that Lindsay Anderson had also, as we have seen, treated as the fountainhead of British film culture: the London Film Society, established in 1925, the year Hitchcock shot his first two features.[16] As Wollen has written elsewhere, "The Film Society was the jumping-off point for Hitchcock."[17] Though confidently asserted, the evidence for this version of events is not overwhelming. Hitchcock was a seasoned filmmaker by the time the principal influence he is supposed to have absorbed through the Film Society—the films and theories of Pudovkin and Eisenstein, whose influence Wollen sees in "the notorious shower murder montage in *Psycho*"—actually appeared in

London; more recent work on Hitchcock's cinematic education, most notably Charles Barr's "Hitchcock and Early Filmmakers," published in 2011, has focused on the years before the Film Society was founded.[18] The first part of what follows extends this line of enquiry by examining the friendship of Hitchcock and Lejeune, and bringing to light the many parallels between their ways of thinking about film during a crucial passage in Hitchcock's career.

*   *   *   *   *   *

Lejeune and Hitchcock first met around 1923 or 1924: in an article giving the latter year, she wrote that "he was writing and ornamenting sub-titles" at the time, which, given that by 1924 he was doing much more, would suggest the earlier date.[19] Born in 1897 and raised in a milieu in which films "were still considered to be not quite proper," Lejeune had moved to London from Manchester in 1921, the year Hitchcock began working full-time at Famous Players-Lasky's Islington studio.[20] Having studied English at Manchester University, she made the move, with her mother, on the pretext of doing research towards a Ph.D., but in reality to impress upon the London editor of the *Manchester Guardian* the need for a film critic. Her mother, a widow, and the *Guardian*'s owner and editor C.P. Scott, a widower, "seemed to find strength and refreshment in each other's company"; young Caroline had contributed articles before, and Scott provided support.[21] Her first article on film, "The Undiscovered Aesthetic," in part her plea for a job, was published on 11 October 1921. "Shame, however, it is, and black shame," she wrote, "that the finer intelligences, the more perceptive critics, should ignore the need for discovery and allow this young art to mature unworthily for lack of sympathetic guidance."[22] It was this that she would provide. Shortly afterwards the London editor took the hint, and her first column appeared on the first Saturday of 1922.

It was not until the autumn of 1935, by which time she had moved to the *Observer*, that Lejeune's weekly contribution was fully divided into discrete reviews, and in the early years at the *Guardian,* her column "The Week on the Screen" was only occasionally tied to the week's releases. It never aspired to total coverage, and as a result none of Hitchcock's first three films as director received a review; nor did the films by other directors which he worked on before then get much attention; nor did many of the early 1920s films from his list of "Ten Favorite Pictures," published in the *New York Sun* in 1939.[23] It was not until 1927, the year his first six films were either released, or had their first runs, or both, that Lejeune mentioned Hitchcock by name. And yet her writings in the pivotal half-decade leading up to this moment, as Hitchcock made his rapid ascent to the director's chair, first at Famous Players-Lasky, then in Michael Balcon's various companies, provide an incomparable guide to the film culture in which he was formed—a film culture that preceded the Film Society and *Close Up*. Not only that, but Lejeune's views from the early 1920s, given on most of the stock themes still familiar to readers of film journalism today, may be shown frequently to have corresponded with those given by Hitchcock both in his British period and much later, in the well-known interviews of the 1960s.

In her first year, Lejeune wrote on such central topics as film authorship, national cinema, art and commerce, acting and stardom, film's relationship with other media, and literary adaptation. In February 1922, for example, in her second month as a columnist, she warned directors against making "actionless thought problems" like John Galsworthy's recent play *The Skin Game* as silent films, "in which the idea to be expressed requires verbal, not visual, media," applying what would become Hitchcock's injunction against "photographs of people talking" to a play he would adapt as a talkie.[24]

The introduction of film critics into British newspapers after the Great War—the *Guardian* had in fact experimented with one a few years before Lejeune's arrival—was in part the result of a felt need to support British film production. Lejeune, however, would not have dissented from Hitchcock's characterization of the British cinema of the 1920s, given in his interview with Truffaut, as "very mediocre; they were mostly for local consumption and were made by bourgeois."[25] In 1922 she deplored British filmmakers' collective lack of "kinema thinking,"[26] and the following year wrote that

> There is no conspicuous fault to be found in the average British film. It is merely flat and unprofitable in story, acting, photography, lighting, and titling— uneasy, indistinct. . . . The best it can offer is a glimpse of some beautiful English scenery, but even our own country looks far more beautiful when an American comes over and "shoots" it.[27]

Lejeune, like most serious film critics of the 1920s, was entirely accustomed to treating films "as the works of a single creative mind," and routinely discussed directors as authors, none more so than D.W. Griffith, who visited London in the spring of 1922 to promote *Orphans of the Storm* (1921), and left a lasting impression on her thought, as we shall see. It was after interviewing Griffith that Lejeune said that the name of the director was "the one name all-important, more vital than the firm for whom he is working, more vital than the 'star' herself," that the star "is merely an instrument in the producer's hands"—like cattle, one might say—and that "Every film should be an expression of the producer's ideal."[28] Likewise Hitchcock, in his first known newspaper article, "Films We Could Make," published in November 1927, wrote that "when moving pictures are really artistic they will be created entirely by one man."[29] In the article he published on Griffith in 1931, "A Columbus of the Screen," Hitchcock repeated Lejeune's contention that the viewing public "rarely lifts aside the thick veil before which the players perform to catch a glimpse of the personality behind."[30] Reviewing her first year in the job at the end of 1922, Lejeune identified "a new, though still feeble, impulse to look upon the making of motion pictures as an art and not as a business," and named a number of directors "who will some day be the artists of the new kinema," including Victor Sjöström, Mauritz Stiller, Marcel L'Herbier, Erich von Stroheim, and Rex Ingram.[31]

In parallel with this proto-auteurist line, however, Lejeune was already advancing what would become one of the major arguments of such auteur-skeptics as Pauline Kael and Raymond Durgnat forty years later. In April 1923, a year after Griffith's visit, she wrote that once a director has an "Olympian" reputation, he or she can never lose it: "Never mind what he may do or leave undone, never mind how trivial his later work, the gloss of reputation will give it a specious brightness."[32] His acolytes, she continued, will discover in his works "subtleties entirely of their own imagining." She had in mind "an audience which was determined to discover at least a moment of excitement in Griffith's 'One Exciting Night,' rejoicing when some innocent discerned the master's touch in the storm suspense scene of the climax."

Lejeune's very first column included a review of Sjöström's *The Phantom Carriage*, aka *Thy Soul Shall Bear Witness* (1921). Before there was a firm conception of "art cinema," Swedish films were treated as qualitatively different by most critics including Lejeune, but were in ordinary commercial distribution, and released without the support of an institutional film culture in which they could be adequately discussed. Similarly, Lejeune attended to the small number of French films that reached London in these years, and was familiar with Louis Delluc's magazine *Cinéa*, whose contributors included Jean Epstein and Jean Cocteau, "the only film paper I have yet encountered which it is an unmixed pleasure to read and whose criticisms are fearless and subtle."[33] More significant for Hitchcock, and indeed for the development of British film culture, however, was the arrival of the first German films, beginning with Ernst Lubitsch's *Passion*, aka *Madame DuBarry* (1919), towards the end of Lejeune's first year on the *Guardian*, in November 1922. After another year had passed, she wrote that "Nineteen hundred and twenty-three will be remembered in the kinema as the German year."[34]

So began the decisive period in Hitchcock's formation as an artist. It is true that he went to Germany in the autumn of 1924 and saw Murnau at work, but by then many of the best-known German films had been released in London; and it has never in any case been demonstrated that he actually saw Fritz Lang's or F.W. Murnau's films while out there, though it is a fair supposition.[35] At any rate, he had seen German films well before they were shown at the Film Society. "My first intimation of the German riches," Lejeune exaggerated in her autobiography, "came on a day when I was invited to an underground theatre in Wardour Street to watch 135 reels of *Dr. Mabuse*, and advise whether they could be cut in such a way as to make a single feature film for British exhibition."[36] She had to ward off the unwanted advances of the sales agent to reach the conclusion. By the end of January of 1923, about the time Hitchcock first became associated with Balcon, Lejeune had seen both *Dr. Mabuse* (1922) and what must have been another of the seminal influences on Hitchcock (though he seldom mentioned either of them by name), Robert Wiene's *The Cabinet of Dr. Caligari* (1920).

By June, a month after *Mabuse*'s London opening, and not long after Sjöström's departure for Hollywood, Lejeune was willing to say that within Europe "we find only one film-producing country of any importance to-day, and that is Germany. Italy is a once-upon-a-time; France is a may-be, Sweden a has-been, and England not at all."[37] It was primarily the German example which led her to revive the search for the "undiscovered aesthetic" which she had gone into film criticism to find. The Germans and French, she wrote in August 1923,

> discovered those things which could be done by the motion-picture and by no other medium of expression, and followed them up to their logical conclusions. Here is an ingenious method, for making untruth visible, they said, for playing havoc with time and space. It is the only medium which can

show to the naked eye those things which do not exist for the naked eye to perceive. It is a liar. It should glory in its lies.[38]

This is surely not far from what Hitchcock himself believed, or came to believe: not only the faith in "pure cinema," but also in outright artifice. "The placing of the images on the screen, in terms of what you're expressing, should never be dealt with in a factual manner," he told Truffaut; "film can be used either to contract time or to extend it at will, in accordance with our needs."[39]

From a Hitchcockian perspective, one of the most remarkable articles Lejeune ever wrote appeared in December 1923, on the subject of staircases, especially German staircases. In this she wrote:

> The staircases of the German films are almost terribly alive and individual. Mystery is the heritage of the species, but the steps in "Dr. Mabuse" have a darker mystery quite their own. The spiral stairs of "The Golem" are furtive and cunning, and the jagged ledges of "Caligari" speak of a world gone mad. There is a certain stairway in the shaft of Pharaoh's tomb [in Lubitsch's *Loves of the Pharaoh* (1922)] at once majestic and cold, while no one who has seen [probably Edmund Löwe's] "Don Juan" will forget the final picture of the wounded man, impotent for the first time in his career, passing slowly down the steps of the palace, a solitary black dot on a vast white incline.[40]

Staircases would of course feature prominently in many of Hitchcock's films, but this last image in particular instantly brings to mind *The Lodger* (1926). More remarkably still, in this same article Lejeune credited Lang's *Destiny* (1921), one of the few German films Hitchcock praised by name, as having "perhaps the most complete apotheosis of the staircase yet screened."[41] In the spring of 1924, when Lang came to London for the opening of *The Nibelungs* (1924), as *Siegfried*, the first part of the *Nibelungen* saga, was titled in Britain, Lejeune interviewed him and learned that *Destiny* was his favorite among his own films, that it had "had to be shown as he made it—or not at all," and that he had had it "hawked round Berlin unavailingly for two years before he found anyone sufficiently enlightened to realise its possibilities."[42] In the same spirit, and rather ironically to modern readers, he reflected on where the line might be drawn: " 'The real difference,' said Fritz Lang, 'lies in the creative artist himself, who can only give what is in him. I myself, for instance, would never dream of making a cowboy film for America.' " It was a few months after this that Hitchcock travelled to Germany to work on Graham Cutts's *The Blackguard* (1925), and by his own account had Lang's great *Nibelungen* sets taken down.

That summer, Lejeune again took a stand against the mindless patriotism then afflicting British film criticism, writing that "the British film industry is a mere pinprick on the face of the film production of the world, just as the kinema is still a pinprick, made by perhaps just a dozen films in all, on the face of the world's art."[43] By then she had almost certainly met the young Hitchcock. "It was obvious to everyone except the commercial nabobs of the industry that some day he would direct pictures, and direct them supremely well," she recalled a decade later.[44] British films, she had written earlier in 1924, were "pallid, insignificant," and had "no breadth of canvas."[45] Of her new friend, on the other hand, she recollected that "All his instincts were towards visualisation, and all his training towards draughtsmanship."[46] Hitchcock for his part, writing in 1936, complained that "There is not enough visualizing done in studios, and instead far too much writing."[47]

It was visualization—"visioning and making visual"— that Lejeune prized in the film Hitchcock saw being shot at Neubabelsberg while working on *The Blackguard*, Murnau's *The Last Laugh*, which opened in London in March 1925, shortly before Hitchcock returned to Germany to make his first feature, *The Pleasure Garden* (1926).[48] "To make a film of the true, the right kinema," she wrote in the week Murnau's film came out, "many artists, of many arts, must be called together. A man of line, a man of rhythm, a man of form, a man of colour, a man of light, a man of movement, a man of mass."[49] Hitchcock, who would write two years later, in "Films We Could Make," about making "a lovely film of rhythmic movement and light and shade," was all of these men; so was Lang.[50] In the autumn of 1925, a few weeks before the first Film Society screening, Lejeune devoted a full column to the latter on the grounds that he was one of the few directors to have realized "that this medium is not only one of movement consecutive in time, but of pose simultaneous in space; that it borrows something from the painter's as well as the dancer's art."[51] Again in "Films We Could Make," Hitchcock wrote that film as a medium of expression "approaches nearest to music and the ballet," and looked longingly to Germany and to the director, presumably Lang's collaborator Walter Ruttmann, whose abstract films resembled "a Cubist painting in motion."[52]

From 1925 at the latest, there is a temptation to imagine that Lejeune was continuing a conversation with Hitchcock in print. In November that year, another of Hitchcock's critic friends, Walter Mycroft of the *Evening Standard*, revealed that Hitchcock's unnamed next film would be, like *The Last Laugh*, "without sub-titles."[53] In April 1926, while Hitchcock was shooting the film in question, *The Lodger*, Lejeune, in a two-column series about the title-less film that used the latterly Hitchcockian phrase "pure kinema," wrote that "the elimination of the sub-title, a favorite device with young producers, seems to be mere folly."[54] Recalling that Griffith had told her that "he considered sub-titles to be quite unnecessary," she likened the practice to "a child hurrying along the pavement with a grim determination not to tread on any of the lines between the stones."[55] Five years earlier, in his first known article on film, published in *Motion Picture Studio*, a spin-off of the trade journal *Kinematograph Weekly* intended for filmmakers, Hitchcock had written in favor of "Art titling," arguing that "illustration gives colour to the action of the story and helps to space the episodes"; and in the event *The Lodger* had titles.[56]

Hitchcock's pure cinema would come to be strongly associated with the idea of montage, usually said to have come to him through the influence of Ivor Montagu, youthful chairman of the Film Society, which began to show the films of Pudovkin and Eisenstein in the autumn of 1928, and translator of Pudovkin's *Film Technique*, which included a description of the "Kuleshov effect," later reconstructed by Hitchcock as a segment in his CBC television interview with Fletcher Markle, "A Talk With Hitchcock," in 1964. Whether Hitchcock had seen any Soviet films before 1928 is unknown, but he could have read about them in Lejeune's column. She was one of the first British critics to see *Battleship Potemkin* (1925), having travelled to Berlin in the summer of 1926 and "caught it by accident one afternoon in some flea-pit in the workers' quarter."[57] Her first report, though it hailed Eisenstein as "undeniably a man of dark genius," praised not its editing but its orchestration of multiple movements within the frame.[58] Intriguingly, another film personality she praised for his sense of movement in the same column was Kuleshov's test-subject, Mosjoukine—doubly intriguingly because Alexandre Volkoff's *Kean* (1924), in which Mosjoukine had starred, had earlier marked an epiphany in her fitful engagement with the aesthetics of editing.

This engagement had begun in March 1923, a couple of months after the appearance of Alma Reville's article "Cutting and Continuity" in *Motion Picture Studio*, a magazine Lejeune certainly read. Reville had written that "The art of cutting is Art indeed, with a capital A," and accused "Mr. Producer" of neglecting it.[59] "Nobody," wrote Lejeune, rallying to the call in the much more widely read *Guardian*, "has really mastered the art of film-cutting as yet. For an art it is, and needs a touch as sure and an instinct as swift as [that] demanded—but rarely won, alas!—from the producer himself."[60] Whether or not Lejeune and Reville had met by this time, the resemblances between the two articles are impossible to miss. *Kean* arrived in London a year later, at what might qualify as London's first art cinema, the Holborn Embassy, which operated as a specialist venue for a few months in the spring of 1924. Lejeune had seen Volkoff's film in a "shabby little picture-house in the artisan quarter of Paris," and spent a full column reviewing it, paying special attention to "the tavern scene, with its chopped, giddy technique, flashing faster and wilder as the dance grows warm," and lamenting that "the gentlemen who sit in Wardour Street" had rejected it.[61] When it opened in May, giving Hitchcock ample opportunity to see it, she called it "the true kinematic film," writing that its virtue "lies in its rhythm, its continuous movement, and the complete dependence of each vision upon the visions that precede and follow it."[62]

It is therefore surprising that her interest in rhythm, which resurfaced in subsequent columns, was not obviously engaged when she first saw *Potemkin*. But it was very much in evidence when, not long afterwards, she finally got around to composing her first article about the director she now counted as a friend, shortly after the general release of his first and third films, *The Pleasure Garden* and *The Lodger*, in March 1927. In this epochal piece of writing, Lejeune asked whether cutting and assembling "signifies anything to us other than a general tidying-up of odds and ends of celluloid, if we realise in the least how structural the final stages of film-making can be."[63] Having described for the uninitiated the practice of "photographing from a dozen angles to find the one right angle for his scene," and having credited Griffith with the "perception of the way in which cutting and assembling could be turned to dramatic purpose," and thereby bringing "the suspense scene into the kinema," she claimed that the "most recent application of cutting and assembling as a dramatic factor has been to the subordinate parts of modern serious films; to the moments of connecting action which were once given up to the sub-title." And she went on to say:

> The modern film describes nothing—it hints, suggests, sketches, flashes from expression to expression, combines three or four images in one. . . . When the producer of "The Lodger" wants to create a sense of dark mystery for his theme he opens with a

series of cuts and flashes of mouths screaming, faces horrified and distorted, newspaper telegrams, rushing news-vans, words on a sky sign, words across the ether, all sorts of startled images.

This method, this "school of jostled vision," she concluded, "in spite of its kinship with modern painting, literature, and stagecraft, is peculiarly the kinema's own." In 1931, when *The Lodger*'s opening reel was shown at the Film Society alongside the auction room scene from *The Skin Game* (1931), she wrote that "It has its own montage, shaped by Hitchcock for his purpose before ever montage became a fashionable term."[64] Simultaneously Lejeune had discovered her aesthetic, and discovered a British director who had mastered it.

* * * * * *

A few months later, in June 1927, shortly after the general release of *The Mountain Eagle* (1926) and the trade show of *Downhill* (1927) on successive days, Lejeune wrote what is very probably Hitchcock's first full profile article in any newspaper, titled "Britain's Baby." Youth was the keynote. "He is more or less new to the kinema; such traditions as he reveres are of the post-German unrepresentational school, and he has never had to go through the shops of commercial hack-work nor adapt himself to a changing technique."[65] She was already prepared to call Hitchcock "the best producer in England," and *The Lodger* "the best film made in England up to the end of last year. It had power, point, imagination, and an entirely new angle—new, that is to say, in an English studio—of visual expression." Despite the plaudits it had won, she doubted that "the British film trade, nor, for that matter, the British film public, has any real estimate of his quality." And yet she too had doubts, which would resurface throughout the next three decades and more. She thought *Downhill* "an interesting production of rubbish," and Hitchcock susceptible to "the modern delusion that it is enough for an artist to give a perfect expression of any subject"; she wanted from him "a picture that is as good in its conception as in its execution."

Ironically, or perhaps knowingly, she also wrote that "I should be astounded to find him producing best-sellers either graciously or well," and possibly as a consequence she managed not to review *The Farmer's Wife* (1928) or *The Manxman* (1929), respectively based on an enormously popular play and a best-selling novel. In her view it was *Blackmail* (1929) which revealed Hitchcock "for the first time in his career as a man who can appreciate human relations and values," though her initial review was not very favorable.[66] *Juno and the Paycock* (1929) she considered filmed theatre, "a production apart from the real nature of the screen," and did not mention Hitchcock's name in connection with it; he was later of the same opinion, telling Truffaut "it had nothing to do with cinema."[67] *Murder!* (1930) had something to do with cinema, but—the complaint was already becoming familiar—not enough to do with life, or "human understanding." In it, "the director, liberated from himself, is able at last to treat his players as choral puppets"—or cattle?—"and to give the technique, which has always been his first concern, first place."[68] But this was not nothing; indeed, Lejeune risked contradicting herself six months later in asking that he escape "the trammels of literary association."[69] Hitchcock knew where he stood, having begun his 1928 article "An Autocrat of the Film Studio" with the statement: "The most important development of the film will be its entire severance from both the stage and the novel, and the command of a medium of its own."[70] It is possible that Lejeune's notion of "human understanding" was ultimately more literary than Hitchcock's, and that his puppetry reflected a kind of human understanding that was alien to her; but her complaints were not simply intended to belittle him as a "popular entertainer."

Lejeune rarely referred to their friendship in print, but scraps from their table talk surfaced in her columns from time to time. In a column of 1932 that treated Hitchcock, Anthony Asquith, and Michael Powell as Britain's leading feature directors, she wrote:

Listen to Hitchcock detailing his first script for "Rich and Strange," with the same clerks, the same babies, the same rush-hour, the same deadly monotony the world over, and you will understand what these men might do for the British screen.[71]

On another occasion, four years before Hitchcock himself described it in his book chapter on "Direction," she wrote of his plans to make "a film of Derby Day."[72] Their first formal interview came in 1932, when Hitchcock, his career at a low ebb, was production supervisor for a brief time at British International Pictures. Loyally but improbably, Lejeune called him "the right man for the job" on the basis of his wide experience, but the bulk of the interview was taken up with his views on synchronized sound, to which he was still adjusting, and related matters:

"I have to screw myself up," he told me the last time we met, "to see a film like `Le Million,' or anything I know I should admire—I am so afraid of unconsciously imitating the director's style, being influenced by it against my will."[73]

Throughout these years, difficult for Hitchcock and difficult for Britain, Lejeune's writing both about him and about British cinema took on a rather boosterish character. She talked up *Waltzes from Vienna* (1934) during production mostly as a praiseworthy exercise in budget-paring, and commended the resulting film as "good enough to make us wish that someone would take the Big Boy of the British studios in hand and force him to take his share in the week-in, week-out drive of British production."[74] After this time in the relative wilderness, Hitchcock returned to Balcon, and Lejeune regained her critical scruples—after a fashion. She greeted *The Man Who Knew Too Much* (1934) as a comeback film precisely because by making a "good, thick-ear melodrama" Hitchcock had "thrown critics and intellectuals overboard with one of his incomparable rude gestures."[75] *The 39 Steps* (1935), exactly six months later, "at last" confirmed her belief, formed at the time of *The Lodger*, that he "would eventually come out on top of all the British-born directors in this country."[76]

Towards the end of 1935, Lejeune wrote a new profile titled "A Genius of the Films," in which she addressed for the first time their "ten-year friendship" (and eleven-year acquaintance).[77] The article augured a new phase in her career, and played a role in a new phase in Hitchcock's. In December it was reprinted in the *New York Times*, *The 39 Steps* having become his breakthrough picture in the U.S. that autumn. Lejeune's relatively personal view, retitled "Meet Alfred Hitchcock" and published before Hitchcock had visited the U.S., must have helped establish what would become the familiar features of his public persona there, especially his way with actors: "Off the set, he is many people's angel. On, he is frequently a fiend."[78] The profile's publication in New York gave Lejeune herself a measure of transatlantic status: a little over two years later, she began writing a monthly column for the *Times*, which she continued through the war and into the late 1940s, sometimes discussing her by-then mostly absent friend.

Sabotage arrived at the end of 1936. In Lejeune's account, she and Hitchcock had observed their "long-standing custom" of going for a meal after the first screening, but because she did not like it, and because he "never tries to persuade the Press against their conscience," *Sabotage* was not discussed.[79] Her review was by no means as negative as has been made out: "There is no department of the industry, script-writing, direction, cutting, sound, and camera, that could not learn something from this picture," she wrote. But in her opinion, "there is a code in this sort of free-handed slaughter, and Hitchcock has gone outside the code." Despite her later reputation, these were not the complaints of an outsider, appalled by thrillers in general, but those of a specialist in the genre, however wrong-headed she may appear now.

When Hitchcock returned with *Young and Innocent* (1937), she claimed victory, writing that he had "reformed, or mellowed, or weakened, or whatever you like to call it."[80] Moreover, she took credit, and claimed that, according to Alma Reville, Hitchcock's assistant Joan Harrison, and the man himself, Hitchcock "blames me for his change of heart. He was pained, it seems, by my comments on his last picture," and changed tack as a consequence. Nor was this a local or temporary affair. When Frank S. Nugent reviewed the film for the *New York Times* a few months later, he quoted Lejeune's review at length, brooding on "the influence of the London reviewer," and the story was repeated in the *Times*'s next major Hitchcock profile, "Hitchcock, Master Melodramatist," in June 1938, with fresh quotes from Lejeune, the paper's recent hire.[81]

Lejeune called *Young and Innocent* her favorite among Hitchcock's films, and held that "it has something which I have missed so far from all the brilliant row of Hitchcock's pictures, and that is humanity."[82] Having explained his predilection for crime stories with a reference to his childhood, when "one of his worst punishments was to be locked up, in a friendly way of course, for a few minutes in the local constabulary," she argued that "for the first time in one of his pictures, the crime is secondary to a warm human interest." However, she clarified that by humanity—"human understanding" she had once called it—she did not mean anything "soft" or "sentimental." Hitchcock's human interest, in this case, lay in "clear-eyed, rather ruthless young people," and in the question "just how far emotion can affect behaviour." It is arguable that, having seen her friend carry out the ambitions she had long nursed for him—making a picture as good in its conception as in its execution—she never engaged with a subsequent Hitchcock film as closely.

Later in the same year Lejeune called *The Lady Vanishes* (1938) "possibly the best, almost certainly the most successful, of all his pictures," and *Rebecca* (1940) two years after that "the Hitchcock film we have been waiting for" and "the best whole that Hitchcock has ever made."[83] But some of the intensity of interest had gone, and not simply because her friend had by the time of the latter film crossed the Atlantic. Indeed, this had long been anticipated. As far back as 1927, she had written that "I am quite certain from the fact that he is still working in this country that the America[n] kinema knows nothing about him at all."[84] At first she appeared to cheer the move. When *Foreign Correspondent* (1940) debuted a few months after *Rebecca,* she wrote that "like Lubitsch alone of Europe's great directors, Hitchcock has found in the New World the full flowering of his talents," and even called his British films "brilliant tentatives" next to the two "mature works" he had made in Hollywood.[85] But these compliments tripped all too easily off the tongue: very rapidly, Lejeune's attitude changed, and never changed back.

At the outbreak of war, Hitchcock had invited Lejeune and her journalist husband Edward Roffe Thompson to join him in California, saying that he could probably find her employment on an American magazine. As she recalled, "It was the action of a true friend, and I still remember the heaviness of heart with which I walked the mile to the nearest post office and sent back a refusal."[86] Their friendship apparently endured. According to her son Anthony, Hitchcock "sent her, every year at Christmas until she died, two dozen half-bottles of champagne."[87] Lejeune herself remembered that "After every London press show of a Hitchcock film I would get a telephone call from Hollywood. 'What did you think about it; honest, kid?' "[88] But one has to wonder how much honesty he could stand. *Mr. and Mrs. Smith* (1941), she wrote, was "likely to be classed amongst the 'and other works' when the large director's biography comes to be written"; *Spellbound* (1945) was "nonsense of a high technical order"; *Notorious* (1946) was "a bit of beautiful nonsense" (though closer to Hitchcock's heart, she felt, than most of his American work); *The Paradine Case* (1947) was "a rather creaky old melodrama"; and *Under Capricorn* (1949) "rather embarrassing to watch."[89] While she took *Shadow of a Doubt* (1943) more seriously, seeing it as properly Hitchcockian, meaning "a story in which the security of middle-class life is savaged by fearful crime," her review was still only lukewarm.[90]

A kind of watershed was reached with her review of *Strangers on a Train* (1951), which she began by recapitulating Griffith's contribution to cinematic suspense, as she had done in her first article on Hitchcock almost a quarter of a century earlier. In both pieces she mentioned Griffith's debt to Dickens, which Griffith had certainly discussed with journalists during the 1922 London trip, possibly with Lejeune herself.[91] In 1927 she had written that "Griffith's peculiar cunning in timing and alternating the various bits of his story, his use of contrast and comparison, were responsible for the success of a school of melodrama which for many years dominated the American screen."[92] By 1951, however, she felt that "all the novelty of the method, and a great deal of the effect, has begun to be rubbed off."[93] Hitchcock's return to it after the experiments of the late 1940s did not win her support. "The old Griffith trick of cross-cutting for suspense," she wrote, "is used to saturation point; in the sense that it absorbs all; except, perhaps, the audience." Their relationship had come full circle.

The irony of the assault on Lejeune by *Sequence* and *Sight and Sound* critics in these years is that their perspective on Hitchcock was almost identical with hers. Published in the Autumn 1949 *Sequence*, Lindsay Anderson's "Alfred Hitchcock," among the first thorough retrospective essays on his work, largely reproduces the perspective that Lejeune had created week by week over the preceding decades: the presaging of "later developments" in *The Lodger*; the dip in quality between *Blackmail* and *The Man Who Knew Too Much*; the high valuation of the 1930s thrillers, "works of art (however minor) because they attain a perfect, satisfying balance between content and style"; and the low valuation of the "glossy photography, high-toned settings, lushly hypnotic musical scores" of 1940s Hollywood, redeemed only by *Shadow of a Doubt*.[94] Indeed, Anderson's praise for the latter exactly echoed Lejeune: whereas she wondered whether "Hitchcock has been taking an intensive course of Orson Welles," on account of the "overlapping dialogue, unrelated conversation carried on between several people at one time," Anderson found "a technique similar to Orson Welles in *The Magnificent Ambersons*, superimposing one conversation over another, dovetailing, naturalistically blurring and distorting."[95]

Lejeune and Anderson's shared perspective on Hitchcock became that of *Sight and Sound* and of its sister publication *Monthly Film Bulletin* through the 1950s. If, as Kapsis says, for "the more intellectual" American critics at this time, "the restraint and understatement of the 'British Hitchcock' were clearly superior to the high-gloss excesses of the 'Paramount Hitchcock,' " for their British equivalents what was really preferred was not the old restraint, if restraint it had been, but the old style.[96] As Gavin Lambert wrote in 1950, "The good, early Hitchcock films were fast, economical, and had a pace and rhythm built on sharp, dramatic cutting."[97] Or as Lejeune put it in her review of the "serious, slow, and non-sensational"—all too restrained, in other words—*The Wrong Man* (1957), "The Hitchcock line is garnished truth, chill fun, sudden shock, ironic contrast, blood on daisies."[98] From this judgment it followed that, after years of disappointment, the crop-dusting scene from *North By Northwest* (1959), the last film of his that she reviewed before *Psycho*, was "likely to be remembered as a classic. For drama, suspense, colour and sheer cinema thrill Hitchcock has never done anything to excel it."[99]

* * * * * *

> I must explain what I mean with some care; for, recently, as a means of disparaging Edgar Poe and of invalidating the sincerity of my admiration, an incautious critic used the word "entertainer," which I had myself applied to this noble poet almost in praise.
> —Baudelaire, "Further Notes on Edgar Poe"[100]

One difficulty with the neat distinction Kapsis and others make between "serious artist" and purveyor of "entertaining 'little British comedy thrillers' "—an unattributed quotation—is revealed in a publication that Kapsis rightly treats as a milestone in the making of Hitchcock's reputation as the former. "The sort of movies he makes," wrote Peter Bogdanovich in the first pages of his MoMA interview book, " —thrillers, mysteries, macabre comedies, suspense films—are considered by American critics as lowbrow and non-art. In England, the genre is a sophisticated, respected one."[101] Bogdanovich probably had Hitchcock's word for it: in the interview, Hitchcock told him that "I had a terrible job casting the thriller-suspense films in America, because over here this kind of story was looked on as second-rate. In England, they're part of the literature, and I had no trouble casting Donat or anybody else there."[102] Ten years later he told Arthur Knight at greater length that: "In England, you see, crime writing is considered first-class literature. . . . You can go back to Conan Doyle, you know, or Wilkie Collins. Go as far as you like, right up to the present day, crime has always interested the litterateurs."[103]

Hitchcock was right: leaving aside his own favorites like John Buchan, no less a litterateur than T.S. Eliot wrote in a famous 1927 essay on Collins and Dickens that

> Those who have lived before such terms as "highbrow fiction," "thrillers" and "detective fiction" were invented realize that melodrama is perennial and that the craving for it is perennial and must be satisfied. If we cannot get this satisfaction out of what the publishers present as "literature," then we will read—with less and less pretence of concealment—what we call "thrillers."[104]

Two years later he wrote that "I am not sure that Sir Arthur Conan Doyle is not one of the great dramatic writers of his age."[105] Lejeune was not a modernist, but she would have understood the argument. In October 1922, the month Eliot's *The Waste Land* was published, she recalled the reaction to Griffith's *Way Down East* (1920):

> You remember the burst of applause, and the superior being in the seat behind who grumbled "Sheer melodrama"? And you remember, but don't like to

confess it, the leap of your own blood, the emotional response to Anna's awakened passion—a quickening of the pulses which even the famous ice-floe scene can never quite recapture. There is nothing to despise in that moment of reaction. Of course Anna's speech is melodrama; the climax, perfectly placed and subtly prepared, of the master melodramatist's greatest work in this mould. But the stuff of melodrama is not despicable in itself.[106]

There was, then, no great contradiction in the British *Man Who Knew Too Much* being at one and the same time a "good, thick-ear melodrama" and "quite possibly the best picture he has ever made."[107] Lejeune treated *Young and Innocent* as seriously as any film she ever reviewed. There was a sophisticated discourse on thrillers, and she contributed to it. In her 1935 profile she compared Hitchcock with another master of the genre, the author of *The Prisoner of Zenda*. "His genius, like Anthony Hope's," wrote Lejeune, "is in starting excitement with the cracking of the first breakfast egg, buying a first-class ticket from Charing Cross to Ruritania. His films are exciting because they take cognizance of the ideas and inhibitions of everyday."[108] Whether or not she was the first to voice it, this thought, oddly phrased but hardly unserious, underlay much of the "British school" of Hitchcock criticism from Anderson, who characterized Hitchcock's ideal subject as "the story of uncertainty, suspense and horror amid humdrum surroundings," to Durgnat, who saw that in the 1930s thrillers "everyday worlds of familiar foibles and eccentricities momentarily part to reveal grimmer patterns."[109]

Not incidentally, Lejeune, who demonstrated her fascination with Sherlock Holmes on numerous occasions as a critic, wrote the first ever BBC television adaptation of the stories in 1951, before adapting Buchan's Richard Hannay novel *The Three Hostages*—a project Hitchcock definitely contemplated—into a series the following year. It was during the preparation of the Holmes series that Lejeune made her most cogent statement on the question whether thrillers could be art. "Talking of Thrillers," published in January 1950, presents itself as the record of a "desultory discussion" among friends, including a "man in brown who produces business-like television plays" who has to be won round. This accomplished, Lejeune provides a list of the best thrillers that the party could remember, including three of Hitchcock's films—*Blackmail*, *The Lady Vanishes*, and *Shadow of a Doubt*— before attempting "to distinguish the quality in a film thriller," leading to a concluding definition foreshadowed in her earlier writings on Hitchcock. Having described Hitchcock as a master of the genre alongside Lang, she wrote that "it is by the realism of its incidentals against the oddity of its atmosphere that you may know the thriller from the non-thriller."[110]

More than a decade later, Truffaut asked Hitchcock why, instead of adapting "popular or light entertainment novels," he did not adapt "such a major classic as Dostoyevsky's *Crime and Punishment*."[111] In Lejeune's discussion, however, Dostoyevsky is cited as a thriller writer, and it is in this way that the doubter is won over. It should at least be apparent that the lack of an absolute distinction between poet and entertainer, serious art and thriller, is nothing new. Moreover, in considering her ultimate rejection, one summer's day in 1960, of Hitchcock's ultimate thriller, one might paraphrase G.K. Chesterton, a writer Hitchcock admired, and say that to be shocked by what is now routine entertainment may be a serious response to art.

The most intense phase in Lejeune and Hitchcock's relationship was the earliest, when these questions were aired for the first time, when critics sought to recognize cinema as an art-form without reference to precedent, when there was an aesthetic to discover, and finer intelligences to win for the cause. Lejeune's campaign was conducted largely in the periodical press, before the establishment of such mythologized institutions of film culture as the Film Society and *Close Up*, and as a result she did not leave a very tangible legacy. When ideas she had advanced in the early 1920s were put forward as if new by later generations, she was attacked in ignorance by those whom she had anticipated. But it was in this primordial struggle that the Hitchcock we know—the artist and the entertainer—was forged. Lejeune was not the only participant who was known to him: Iris Barry and Walter Mycroft were also in the thick of it. But his friendship with Lejeune was closer and more enduring, and almost certainly more significant; and as a result her testimony across a hundred and more columns is uniquely illuminating. She had encountered in person such titanic figures in Hitchcock's development as Griffith and Lang, and mediated the influence of others such as Eisenstein; she was the standard-bearer for German cinema on its arrival in London; and she was a staunch critic of the native cinema whose confines Hitchcock from the first sought to escape. She articulated what he meant by "pure cinema," even as he was finding his way towards realizing it on screen. On a score of vital questions they were of one mind. However it came about, and whatever happened later, the correspondences would be striking even if they had never met.

Notes

1. Cited in Amanda Sheahan Wells, *Psycho* (London: York Press, 2001), 10.

2. C.A. Lejeune, "Something Nasty in the Motel," *Observer*, 7 August 1960, 19; reprinted in Anthony Lejeune, ed., *The C.A. Lejeune Film Reader* (Manchester: Carcanet, 1991), 302-03.

3. Peter Bogdanovich, *The Cinema of Alfred Hitchcock* (New York: The Museum of Modern Art Film Library, 1963), 19.

4. Patrick McGilligan, *Backstory: Interviews with Screenwriters of Hollywood's Golden Age* (Berkeley and Los Angeles: University of California Press, 1986), 28.

5. Lejeune, "Taking the Plunge," *Observer*, 14 September 1947, 2; "On The Brink," *Observer*, 31 August 1947, 2.

6. Lejeune, "Taking the Plunge," 2.

7. Penelope Houston, rev. of C.A. Lejeune, *Chestnuts in Her Lap*, in *Sequence*, 2 (winter 1947): 33-34; "Leading the Blind," *Sight and Sound* 18, no. 69 (spring 1949): 42-43.

8. Houston, rev. C. A. Lejeune, *Thank You For Having Me*, in *Sight and Sound* 33, no. 2 (spring 1964): 101.

9. Lindsay Anderson, "Stand Up! Stand Up!," *Sight and Sound* 26, no. 2 (autumn 1956): 64.

10. Charles Barr, "Critics," *Granta*, 26 November 1960, 19-22.

11. V.F. Perkins, *Film as Film: Understanding and Judging Movies* (Harmondsworth: Penguin, 1972), 9.

12. Robert E. Kapsis, *Hitchcock: The Making of a Reputation* (Chicago: University of Chicago Press, 1992), 156, 8.

13. Kapsis, *Hitchcock: The Making of a Reputation*, 1.

14. Kapsis, *Hitchcock: The Making of a Reputation*, 103.

15. Kapsis, *Hitchcock: The Making of a Reputation*, 155.

16. Peter Wollen, "Hitch: A Tale of Two Cities," in *Paris Hollywood: Writings on Film* (London: Verso, 2002), 67.

17. Wollen, "Rope: Three Hypotheses," in Richard Allen and S. Ishii-Gonzalès, eds., *Alfred Hitchcock: Centenary Essays* (London: BFI Publishing, 1999), 79.

18. Wollen, "Rope: Three Hypotheses," 78; Charles Barr, "Hitchcock and Early Filmmakers," in *A Companion to Alfred Hitchcock*, ed. Thomas Leitch and Leland Poague (Malden, MA: Wiley Blackwell, 2011), 48-66.

19. Lejeune, "A Genius of the Films: Alfred Hitchcock and His Work," *Observer*, 17 November 1935, 13. "Sub-titles" was a contemporary term for titles or intertitles.

20. Lejeune, *Thank You For Having Me* (London: Hutchinson, 1964), 49. For Hitchcock's dates of employment, see Patrick McGilligan, *Alfred Hitchcock: A Life in Darkness and Light* (Chichester: Wiley, 2003), 46.

21. Lejeune, *Thank You For Having Me*, 37.

22. Lejeune, "The Undiscovered Aesthetic," *Manchester Guardian*, 11 October 1921, 14.

23. Alfred Hitchcock, "My Ten Favorite Pictures," *New York Sun*, 15 March 1939, 33. This curious list, probably discovered by Donald Spoto, includes Cecil B. DeMille's *Forbidden Fruit* (1921) and *Saturday Night* (1922), John S. Robertson's *Sentimental Tommy* (1921) and *The Enchanted Cottage* (1923), Rex Ingram's *Scaramouche* (1923), Maurice Tourneur's *The Isle of Lost Ships* (1923), Charlie Chaplin's *The Gold Rush* (1925), E.A. Dupont's *Vaudeville* (1925), Josef von Sternberg's *The Last Command* (1928), and a single sound film, Mervyn LeRoy's *I Am A Fugitive From a Chain Gang* (1932).

24. Lejeune, "The Test of Truth," *Manchester Guardian*, 25 February 1922, 9.

25. François Truffaut with the collaboration of Helen G. Scott, *Hitchcock,* revised ed. (New York: Simon and Schuster, 1984), 124.

26. Lejeune, "Made in England," *Manchester Guardian,* 10 June 1922, 5.

27. Lejeune, "Seeing Ourselves," *Manchester Guardian,* 7 April 1923, 9.

28. Lejeune, "The Man Behind the Film," *Manchester Guardian,* 22 April 1922, 7. She went on to explain why she preferred the English term "producer" to the American term "director": "the part which he plays in the art of the screen is creative, not merely governing."

29. Hitchcock, "Films We Could Make," *Evening News,* 16 November 1927, 13; reprinted in Sidney Gottlieb, ed., *Hitchcock on Hitchcock: Selected Writings and Interviews* (Berkeley and Los Angeles: University of California Press, 1995), 65-67.

30. Hitchcock, "A Columbus of the Screen," *Film Weekly,* 21 February 1931, 9; reprinted in Sidney Gottlieb, ed., *Hitchcock on Hitchcock: Selected Writings and Interviews, Volume 2* (Berkeley and Los Angeles: University of California Press, 2015), 126-29.

31. Lejeune, "The End of a Chapter," *Manchester Guardian,* 30 December 1922, 5.

32. Lejeune, " 'What Fools These Mortals Be!' " *Manchester Guardian,* 21 April 1923, 9.

33. Lejeune, "'Writing Up' The Kinema," *Manchester Guardian,* 2 September 1922, 7.

34. Lejeune, "1923," *Manchester Guardian,* 29 December 1923, 5.

35. For a thorough accounting of the manifold German influences on Hitchcock, see Sidney Gottlieb, "Early Hitchcock: The German Influence," *Hitchcock Annual* 8 (1999-2000): 100-30.

36. Lejeune, *Thank You For Having Me,* 92.

37. Lejeune, "The Hall-Mark of Race," *Manchester Guardian,* 16 June 1923, 9.

38. Lejeune, "Visible Thought," *Manchester Guardian,* 18 August 1923, 7.

39. Truffaut, *Hitchcock,* 265, 294.

40. Lejeune, "Jacob's Ladder," *Manchester Guardian,* 15 December 1923, 7.

41. Lejeune, "Jacob's Ladder," 7.

42. Lejeune, "The Man Who Made 'Siegfried,' " *Manchester Guardian,* 6 May 1924, 5.

43. Lejeune, "The Patriot," *Manchester Guardian,* 5 July 1924, 9.

44. Lejeune, "A Genius of the Films," 13.

45. Lejeune, "The New Year at Home," *Manchester Guardian*, 5 January 1924, 7.

46. Lejeune, "A Genius of the Films," 13.

47. Hitchcock, "Close Your Eyes and Visualize!" *Stage*, July 1936, 52-53; reprinted in *Hitchcock on Hitchcock*, 247.

48. Lejeune, "Continuity," *Manchester Guardian*, 28 March 1925, 7.

49. Lejeune, "Constructional," *Manchester Guardian*, 21 March 1925, 7.

50. Hitchcock, "Films We Could Make," 13.

51. Lejeune, "A Giant," *Manchester Guardian*, 5 September 1925, 9.

52. Hitchcock, "Films We Could Make," 13.

53. Walter Mycroft, "Features of the Films," *Illustrated Sunday Herald*, 1 November 1925, 19.

54. Lejeune, "Silent Sound," *Manchester Guardian*, 3 April 1926, 9; "The Sphere of the Sub-Title," *Manchester Guardian*, 10 April 1926, 9; reprinted in *The C.A. Lejeune Film Reader*, 77-79.

55. Lejeune, "The Sphere of the Sub-Title," 9.

56. Hitchcock, "Titles—Artistic and Otherwise," *Motion Picture Studio*, 23 July 1921, 6; reprinted in *Hitchcock on Hitchcock, Volume 2*, 71-72.

57. Lejeune, *Thank You For Having Me*, 112.

58. Lejeune, "Trajectory," *Manchester Guardian*, 24 July 1926, 9.

59. Alma Reville, "Cutting and Continuity," *Motion Picture Studio*, 13 January 1923, 10; reprinted with Nathalie Morris's "The Early Career of Alma Reville," in *Hitchcock Annual* 15 (2006-07): 1-34.

60. Lejeune, "Cuts," *Manchester Guardian*, 31 March 1923, 7.

61. Lejeune, " 'Kean,' " *Manchester Guardian*, 22 March 1924, 9. *Kean* was also an important film for Michael Powell, who saw it at the Vieux-Colombier, probably the cinema Lejeune meant, and described the tavern scene as "a brilliant tour-de-force of images, lighting, editing, perhaps one of the most successful dance sequences I have seen filmed. Until *The Red Shoes*." See Michael Powell, "Michael Powell's Guilty Pleasures," *Film Comment* 17, no. 4 (July-August 1981): 31.

62. Lejeune, "Still Life," *Manchester Guardian*, 17 May 1924, 9.

63. Lejeune, "The Week on the Screen," *Manchester Guardian*, 5 March 1927, 11.

64. Lejeune, "The Old and the New: 'The Lodger' and 'The Skin Game,' " *Observer*, 1 March 1931, 12.

65. Lejeune, "Britain's Baby," *Manchester Guardian*, 11 June 1927, 9.

66. Lejeune, "A Big Three," *Observer*, 28 July 1929, 11.

67. Lejeune, "Fine Speech," *Observer*, 5 January 1930, 13; Truffaut, *Hitchcock*, 69.

68. Lejeune, "Hitchcock and 'Murder,'" *Observer*, 10 August 1930, 9. Both the phrase and the argument were reused in Lejeune's discussion of Hitchcock in her book *Cinema* (London: Alexander Maclehouse, 1931), 10-13.

69. Lejeune, "The Old and the New: 'The Lodger' and 'The Skin Game,'" 12

70. Hitchcock, "An Autocrat of the Film Studio," *Cassell's Magazine*, January 1928, 28; reprinted in *Hitchcock on Hitchcock, Volume 2*, 116-23.

71. Lejeune, "Stars Mean Money," *Observer*, 31 January 1932, 12.

72. Lejeune, "The Drama Round Us," *Observer*, 4 June 1933, 10; Alfred Hitchcock, "Direction," in Charles Davy, ed., *Footnotes to the Film* (London: Lovat Dickson, 1937), 4; reprinted in *Hitchcock on Hitchcock*, 253-61.

73. Lejeune, "The Difficulties of Dialogue," *Observer*, 21 August 1932, 16.

74. Lejeune, "'Waltzes From Vienna,'" *Observer*, 22 October 1933, 24; "Directors Wanted," *Observer*, 4 March 1934, 25.

75. Lejeune, "The Man Who Knows Enough," *Observer*, 9 December 1934, 12.

76. Lejeune, "A British Film To See," *Observer*, 9 June 1935, 10; reprinted in *The C.A. Lejeune Film Reader*, 96-97.

77. Lejeune, "A Genius of the Films," 13.

78. Lejeune, "Meet Alfred Hitchcock," *New York Times*, 15 December 1935, X7. It is probably from this profile that the tale of his habit of smashing teacups derives.

79. Lejeune, "One For All, And All For One," *Observer*, 6 December 1936, 14; reprinted in *The C.A. Lejeune Film Reader*, 106-07.

80. Lejeune, "Hitchcock on Youth and Innocence," *Observer*, 30 January 1938, 12; reprinted in *The C.A. Lejeune Film Reader*, 120-22.

81. Frank S. Nugent, "Pictures in Review," *New York Times*, 20 February 1938, X5; B.R. Crisler, "Hitchcock: Master Melodramatist," *New York Times*, 12 June 1938, X3.

82. Lejeune, "Hitchcock on Youth and Innocence," 12.

83. Lejeune, "The Misadventures of Robin Hood," *Observer*, 9 October 1938, 16; reprinted in *The C.A. Lejeune Film Reader*, 129-30; "'Rebecca'," *Observer*, 30 June 1940, 11. In the weekly *Sketch*, another London paper she wrote for at this time, Lejeune called *Rebecca* "in every way his best" (*Sketch*, 10 July 1940, 52).

84. Lejeune, "Britain's Baby," 9.

85. Lejeune, "Hitchcock and the Field," *Observer*, 13 October 1940, 11; reprinted in *The C.A. Lejeune Film Reader*, 171-72.

86. Lejeune, *Thank You For Having Me*, 165.

87. Anthony Lejeune, "Preface," in *The C. A. Lejeune Film Reader*, 15.

88. Lejeune, *Thank You For Having Me*, 165.

89. Lejeune, "Various Victories," *Observer*, 30 March 1941, 3 (on *Mr. And Mrs. Smith*); "The Films," *Observer*, 19 May 1946, 2; reprinted in *The C.A. Lejeune Film Reader*, 187 (on *Spellbound*); "Six In Hand," *Observer*, 16 February 1947, 2 (on *Notorious*); "Germany Calling," *Observer*, 16 January 1949, 2 (on *The Paradine Case*); "Female Victims' Week," *Observer*, 9 October 1949, 6; reprinted in *The C.A. Lejeune Film Reader*, 242-43 (on *Under Capricorn*).

90. Lejeune, "The Films," *Observer*, 28 March 1943, 2; reprinted in Lejeune, *Chestnuts in Her Lap* (London: Phoenix House, 1947), 87-89; and in *The C.A. Lejeune Film Reader*, 228-29.

91. See, for example, A.B. Walkley, "Switching Off," *The Times*, 26 April 1922, 12; cited in S.M. Eisenstein, *Film Form: Essays in Film Theory*, ed. and trans. Jay Leyda (New York: Harcourt, Brace, 1949), 205.

92. Lejeune, "The Week on the Screen," 11.

93. Lejeune, "Tense and Past Tense," *Observer*, 5 August 1951, 6.

94. Lindsay Anderson, "Alfred Hitchcock," *Sequence*, no. 9 (autumn 1949), 115, 123, 119.

95. Lejeune, "The Films," *Observer*, 28 March 1943, 2; Anderson, "Alfred Hitchcock," 121. Orson Welles was in fact an admirer of Hitchcock's 1930s thrillers, and of *Shadow of a Doubt*, to which he paid homage with *The Stranger* (1946).

96. Kapsis, *Hitchcock: The Making of a Reputation*, 45.

97. Gavin Lambert, rev. of *Stage Fright*, in *Monthly Film Bulletin*, no. 197 (June 1950): 82-83.

98. Lejeune, "Fiction and Fact," *Observer*, 24 February 1957, 11. Hitchcock first made reference to this treasured image of "blood on daisies" in 1937. A quarter of a century later, in his interview with Truffaut, he describes "a shot I've always dreamed of: a murder in a tulip field. . . . One petal fills the screen, and suddenly a drop of blood splashes all over it" (Truffaut, *Hitchcock*, 135).

99. Lejeune, "Packaged Thrills," *Observer*, 18 October 1959, 25; reprinted in *The C.A. Lejeune Film Reader*, 301-02.

100. Charles Baudelaire, "Further Notes on Edgar Poe," in Baudelaire, *Selected Writings on Art and Literature*, trans. P.E. Charvet (London: Penguin, 2006), 190.

101. Bogdanovich, *The Cinema of Alfred Hitchcock*, 3.

102. Bogdanovich, *The Cinema of Alfred Hitchcock*, 21.

103. Arthur Knight, "Conversation with Alfred Hitchcock," *Oui*, February 1973; reprinted in Sidney Gottlieb, ed., *Alfred Hitchcock: Interviews* (Jackson: University Press of Mississippi, 2003), 167.

104. T.S. Eliot, "Wilkie Collins and Dickens," *Times Literary Supplement*, 4 August 1927, 525-26; cited in David E. Chinitz, *T.S. Eliot and the Cultural Divide* (Chicago: University of Chicago Press, 2003), 55.

105. Eliot, "Books of the Quarter," *Criterion* 8, no. 32 (April 1929): 556.

106. Lejeune, "Melodrama," *Manchester Guardian*, 28 October 1922, 7. In 1950 Hitchcock told the *New York Times Magazine* that *Way Down East* contained the best chase sequence he had ever seen (*Hitchcock on Hitchcock*, 131).

107. Lejeune, "The Man Who Knows Enough," 12.

108. Lejeune, "A Genius of the Films," 13.

109. Anderson, "Alfred Hitchcock," 114; Raymond Durgnat, *The Strange Case of Alfred Hitchcock* (London: Faber and Faber, 1974), 24.

110. Lejeune, "Talking of Thrillers," *Observer*, 15 January 1950, 6.

111. Truffaut, *Hitchcock*, 69-71.

PAUL HASPEL

California in Extremis: The West Coast Setting and *1960's Anxiety in* The Birds

Since its release, Alfred Hitchcock's 1963 film *The Birds* has commanded the attention of viewers and critics alike. Hitchcock himself once referred to *The Birds*, with its elaborate special effects and innovative sound design, as "the most prodigious job ever done."[1] *The Birds* also stands out among Hitchcock's films as the only one that truly bothered the great director during its production. John Russell Taylor reports that Hitchcock, who usually took pride in "leaving work at the studio and detaching himself completely when he gets home," nonetheless "found himself nervy and oppressed" while making *The Birds*—"possibly because of the kind of subject he was handling, a vision of Judgment Day for humanity, possibly for deeper-laid, more mysterious personal reasons."[2]

Controversial at the time of its release, *The Birds* has over the following half-century found many champions among students of Hitchcock's work. Donald Spoto describes the film as being "among [Hitchcock's] half-dozen masterpieces and one of the purest, most darkly lyrical films ever made," and adds that filmmaker Federico Fellini "called it an apocalyptic poem and affirmed it as his own favorite among Hitchcock's works and one of the cinema's greatest achievements."[3]

One facet of *The Birds* that has not received as much critical attention as other aspects of the film—issues of

gender and psychology, for example—is its California
setting, first in San Francisco and then in the small coastal
town of Bodega Bay. California looms large in the American
imagination, and setting the film there is relevant to specific
themes that Hitchcock is interested in exploring, especially
the overall mood of anxiety. For many, both in the United
States and elsewhere, California embodies a distillation of
American life and the American Dream; it is a kind of
quintessence of U.S. society at its best and worst, the end
point of the westward movement that has been, for many,
characteristic of the American experience. As California
historian Kevin Starr puts it, "There has always been
something bipolar about California. It was either utopia or
dystopia, a dream or a nightmare, a hope or a broken
paranoia—and too infrequently anything in between."[4]
Similarly, Joan Didion writes in *Slouching Towards Bethlehem*
that "California is a place where a boom mentality and a
sense of Chekhovian loss meet in uneasy suspension; in
which the mind is troubled by some buried but ineradicable
suspicion that things had better work here, because here,
beneath that immense bleached sky, is where we run out
of continent."[5]

Hitchcock shared that interest in the idea of California as
a potential expression of the best and the worst in American
life, and explored that theme in *The Birds*. In the film's crucial
Tides Restaurant sequence, as in *The Birds* generally,
Hitchcock, in tandem with screenwriter Evan Hunter,
suggests that the elements that comprise the perceived
California lifestyle—an optimistic, forward-looking quality
that reflects the state's frontier heritage and its location on the
Pacific Ocean; a relaxed appreciation for good living; a
mellow temperament encouraged by the state's mild
climate—mask social divisions and fundamental human
imperfections that impair the community's ability to respond
meaningfully to a crisis situation.

Fear of loss is certainly a preeminent theme of *The Birds*.
William Rothman writes that "*The Birds* and *Marnie*,
[Hitchcock's] two last masterpieces, are infused with a deep

sense of loss, an urgency, and an emotional directness that set them apart from all other Hitchcock films. They declare something about the human need for love that was always implicit in his work."[6] As he had done in *Shadow of a Doubt,* in *The Birds* Hitchcock "destroyed the illusion of rural bliss" in a northern California town, showing "that a placid, pastoral milieu is a surface sign of underlying unrest in terms of escapist fantasy, boredom, seething passions, deviance and, yes, even murder."[7] These themes come forth with particular force in *The Birds* because of the way in which Hitchcock linked the California setting of the film with contemporary concerns over the possibility of an apocalyptic nuclear conflict between the United States and the Soviet Union.

In setting forth these ideas, I do not plan to present a point-by-point correspondence of plot events from *The Birds* with historical events from the Cold War era. John Hellmann's essay "*The Birds* and the Kennedy Era" has already done so in a thorough and effective manner. Additionally, I am not claiming that *The Birds* is, fundamentally, a "Cold War" film. Hitchcock engaged Cold War themes and concerns much more directly in a number of his later films, such as *Torn Curtain* (1966) and *Topaz* (1969). Perhaps most famously, he placed the Cold War at the dramatic and thematic center of *North by Northwest* (1959), particularly when protagonist Roger O. Thornhill (played by Cary Grant) scolds a mysterious spymaster known only as "The Professor" (Leo G. Carroll) for putting a civilian woman, Eve Kendall (Eva Marie Saint), at risk as part of a scheme to capture enemy spy Phillip Vandamm (James Mason). That Cold War element of Hitchcock's work, while interesting, lies outside the scope of this essay.

My interest is in the generalized climate of anxiety that existed throughout much of the post-1945 world regarding the existence of nuclear weapons and the prospect that those weapons might, deliberately or accidentally, be deployed—an anxiety that often was acutely felt not only in major cities like New York or Washington or San Francisco, but also in small towns like Bodega Bay, places far from the seats of power. For

Hitchcock, moreover, this anxiety is deepened by an awareness of the incapacity of most humans to respond rationally and effectively in times of crisis, a sobering fact dramatized repeatedly throughout *The Birds*.

Hitchcock's California, Hitchcock's America: Bright Surface vs. Grim Reality

Bernard Dick suggests that Alfred Hitchcock drew upon Daphne du Maurier's 1952 story "The Birds" because of "a coastal setting, suggesting isolation both geographical and social," and moving the story from Britain's Scilly Islands to Bodega Bay signified "a matter of substituting one insular community for another."[8] By the time he filmed *The Birds*, Hitchcock had been living and working in America for almost two decades. The characters and locales of his post-1940 films were overwhelmingly American, and he dedicated himself to the task of examining and interrogating American culture generally. In their introduction to *Hitchcock's America*, Jonathan Freedman and Richard Millington aptly suggest that "at the center of Hitchcock's Hollywood films stands a sustained, specific, and extraordinarily acute exploration of American culture," to the point that Hitchcock "might be viewed as an indispensable historian, critic, and analyst of American middle-class culture from the 1940s through the 1970s."[9]

Cynthia Freeland suggests that when Hitchcock relocated *The Birds* to California he "set the human/bird conflict within the broader context of American society, downplaying the [British and World War II] atmosphere of the original."[10] This move also demonstrated that Hitchcock was returning to a strategy he had deployed successfully in *Shadow of a Doubt* twenty years earlier: as Irving Singer points out, "In *Shadow of a Doubt*, as in *The Birds*, the routine and uneventful serenity of a small town in California is the calculated setting for the grotesque and egregious evil that descends upon it."[11]

The idea of hideous evil hiding just beneath the surface of a seemingly idyllic social landscape is a consistent feature of many of Hitchcock's California films prior to *The Birds*. In *Shadow of a Doubt*, a serial killer from the East is able to take shelter with family members in Santa Rosa and is quickly accepted by the town as an eminent citizen. When his attempt to kill his own niece goes awry and results in his own death, he is eulogized, ironically, as "a son that [Santa Rosa] can be proud of." *Vertigo* (1958) is set not in a small city like Santa Rosa but rather in the great metropolis of San Francisco. The beauty of the city is captured by Robert Burks's gorgeous Technicolor photography, but beautiful San Francisco is the locale for a very ugly murder, as a wealthy industrialist hatches an elaborate plot to murder his wife, make the murder look like a suicide, and then abscond to Europe to live comfortably off the fruits of his crime. And *Psycho* (1960) returns to rural California, to the fictitious Southern California community of Fairvale, where the polite and cheerful demeanor of the young motel owner Norman Bates (Anthony Perkins) helps him successfully conceal from his fellow townspeople his double life as a serial killer.

The Birds shares the California setting and some of the thematic interests of those three earlier films, but differs in some ways from anything Hitchcock had done previously. In choosing du Maurier's "The Birds" as his literary source, Hitchcock committed himself for the first time to a story with a non-human antagonist. While linking *The Birds* with the genres of science fiction and fantasy, Joel Finler suggests that "the picture also qualifies as a kind of 'disaster movie,' related to the many, generally cheaply made apocalyptic movies of the era."[12] Finler's point regarding the low quality of many films of this genre is valid—he cites Ranald MacDougall's *The World, the Flesh, and the Devil* (1959), Val Guest's *The Day the Earth Caught Fire* (1961), and Ray Milland's *Panic in Year Zero!* (1962) as examples. Even when the great special-effects artist Ray Harryhausen contributed his stop-motion effects to a film of this genre—creating for *It Came From Beneath the Sea* (1955) a giant octopus that is driven out of its deep-sea home by hydrogen-bomb testing, attacks San Francisco, and destroys the Golden Gate Bridge—the result is simply that an otherwise cheap and forgettable film is enlivened by good special effects. Yet it is also true that such films, whatever their quality, expressed a culture-wide anxiety that nuclear weapons could bring an end to all life on earth; and by the time Hitchcock began envisioning the project that became *The Birds*, the genre of apocalyptic science fiction was drawing attention from quality directors who could command first-rate creative teams in well-budgeted films.

Notable among such films was *On the Beach* (1959), a film that demonstrates the extent to which nuclear anxiety affected post-World War II society. Like its literary source, a 1957 novel of the same title by Australian writer Nevil Shute, the plot of *On the Beach* is driven by the fear of nuclear war. The great powers of the Northern Hemisphere have destroyed themselves and each other in a nuclear war, and the residents of Southern Hemisphere nations like Australia can do nothing but wait for the deadly clouds of radiation to drift south. Well-budgeted and well-publicized, *On the Beach* had an A-list director in Stanley Kramer, a filmmaker known for making socially conscious films; a talented cast that included Gregory Peck, Ava Gardner, Fred Astaire, and future *Psycho* star Anthony Perkins; and a crucial scene in which a U.S. Navy submarine sails into San Francisco Bay and moors in front of the Ferry Building on the Embarcadero. Perhaps Hitchcock felt that he, like Kramer, could take a well-worn B-movie genre, work from a source that was respectable but not necessarily "literary," incorporate a California setting, and make something new out of it, just as he had in adapting the Boileau-Narcejac novel *D'entre les morts* into *Vertigo*, and in turning Robert Bloch's *Psycho* into a film so successful that fans and critics alike were asking what Hitchcock could possibly do next.

It seems clear that Hitchcock had *On the Beach* very much on his mind as he worked on *The Birds*. In a 1963 interview, he described *The Birds* as an example of "these films, which I call an 'event' film—you know, like *On the Beach*, or one of those things."[13] Hitchcock built further upon that idea of the "event film" in a later interview in which he said of *The Birds* that "traditionally it's an event story, like the early H.G. Wells stories, like 'War of the Worlds.' "[14] Yet he clearly did not want to emulate *On the Beach* in all respects, telling Peter Bogdanovich in an interview that "I've noticed that in other 'catastrophe' films, such as *On the Beach,* the personal stories were never really part of it at all."[15] It seems clear that Hitchcock wanted to make sure that his own California "catastrophe" film would be a substantial and character-oriented story, not simply an "event film."

Bodega Bay ended up working well as a setting for Hitchcock's storytelling purposes. He said that *The Birds* "needed a present-day atmosphere. And in order to get the photography of the birds in the air, we needed an area with low land, not high mountains or a lot of trees. In a pictorial sense, it was vital to have nothing on the ground but sand so that we had the entire sky to play with. Bodega Bay had all of that."[16] Hitchcock worked hard to take a beautiful, colorful community of coastal California and make it look gray and flat. Hitchcock later said that he "wanted it to be gloomy. It was necessary to subdue the color of many of the scenes in the film lab to get the proper effect." Art director Robert Boyle corroborated this intention, adding that "some of the reviews criticized us for not playing up the beauty of Bodega Bay, but we didn't want it to be colorful. We weren't making a 'Bright Day at Malibu' type of picture."[17]

It is noteworthy that Hitchcock chose for his setting a real-life town rather than an invented locale. Setting the film's apocalyptic action in an actual place that can be located on a map or visited no doubt was intended to make the events of the drama seem more real. Hitchcock worked with Evan Hunter to make sure that *The Birds* would have the dramatic concentration and focus characteristic of his films, as when he reviewed a draft of the script and informed Hunter that "At Bodega Bay, I can clearly see that we do have one or two scenes with no particular shape. . . . I feel sure that these could be eliminated so that the scene when she presents herself at the school teacher's house with a paper bag can be dramatically capitalized."[18]

Once Hitchcock's film crew arrived in Bodega Bay, they "made full use of actual buildings—including the Tides restaurant and a dilapidated schoolhouse which was refurbished for the film—as well as purpose-built facades, among them the Brenner farm and Annie Hayworth's house."[19] In doing so, Hitchcock created his own Bodega Bay that served his own fictive and thematic purposes, just as he had done with the similarly real community of Santa Rosa in *Shadow of a Doubt*. As Hitchcock's interest was in creating his own Bodega Bay, an imaginary location that incorporates elements of geographical reality but is not tethered to that reality, perhaps it would amuse him to know that decades later, when modern-day fans of *The Birds* make a pilgrimage to the Bodega Bay of today, they often find that, even when they try to overlook the changes of almost half a century, nothing in the layout of the modern community seems to match the setup of the town they saw in the film.

San Francisco and Bodega Bay: Contrasts and Commonalities

John Orr sees F.W. Murnau's *Sunrise* (1927) as a powerful influence on Hitchcock generally and *The Birds* specifically. Orr points out that "In *Sunrise* Murnau created an entire social world, a film text as a living organism that links imaginary country to city," although while "*Sunrise* starts in the country then goes to the city . . . In Hitchcock's quintessentially Californian films, *Vertigo* and *The Birds*, he inverts the process with variations."[20] Richard Allen adds that in *Sunrise*, as in *The Birds*, "a woman of the city descends upon a village to seduce a man who lives with his family by the water."[21]

That main action of *The Birds* occurs in Bodega Bay, but the film begins in San Francisco, where the two main characters, Melanie Daniels (Tippi Hedren) and Mitch Brenner (Rod Taylor), both occupy positions of power and influence: Melanie because of her wealth, her high social position, and her status as the daughter of a powerful San Francisco newspaper publisher, and Mitch because of his work as a defense attorney who takes on high-profile criminal cases, like that of a man who shot his wife six times for changing the TV channel during a ball game. The city is depicted as a haven of wealth and sophistication, a center for international travel and commerce.

This positive impression of San Francisco in the film's opening sequence may reflect Hitchcock's own feelings toward the city. Hitchcock's daughter, Patricia, told a biographer that "The first time my father saw San Francisco, he fell in love with it, and throughout his life, he only fell more deeply in love with it. He thought it was very like Paris."[22] Those positive feelings, set forth in the loving detail with which San Francisco is depicted in *Vertigo,* also emerge in this opening sequence of *The Birds.* Perhaps it is for that reason that Hitchcock places his traditional cameo not in the Bodega Bay portion that takes up the major portion of the film's running time, but rather in the brief introductory San Francisco sequence, where he is seen walking his two dogs out of the pet shop that Melanie Daniels is about to enter, although he may also have done so in order simply to get his cameo out of the way as quickly as possible.

Before that pet-shop scene, the viewer first sees Melanie walking through San Francisco's Union Square, an area that a recent travel book aptly describes as "the commercial hub of San Francisco."[23] Another travel guide calls Union Square "the single space uniting the several elements and attitudes of the city. The chic center for the 'shop 'til you drop' set, it is also where pigeons and protesters come to see and be part of the scene."[24] It seems appropriate, therefore, that Union Square is where the wealthy and fashionable Melanie comes to do her bird shopping. Melanie's walk is "located for us in time and space by means of glimpsed travel posters (including one of the Golden Gate Bridge) and airline signs, [and] by familiar [San Francisco] icons" like "a cable-car [and] the Dewey Monument commemorating an event in the Spanish-American War."[25] The Dewey Monument, which salutes a forgotten American victory in an often overlooked American war, may look ahead to what both Mitch Brenner and the

Figure 1. Melanie walking through Union Square. The
Dewey Monument is visible, along with airline signs.

amateur ornithologist Mrs. Bundy will refer to as the "bird
war," a conflict that will not lend itself to memorializing
through marble or granite monuments. In this setting, where
things are ostensibly normal, birds are "excluded, at the
margins of the frame or story."[26] Peter Conrad points out how
"Above Union Square, hoardings for airlines utter siren songs:
JET BOAC TO ALL 5 CONTINENTS, OR AIR FRANCE JET TO PARIS DIRECT
FROM CALIFORNIA–symptoms of the imbalance in nature, now
that planes have stolen the sky from birds."[27] (fig. 1)

In the urban and urbane environment of San Francisco, as
Mitch plays a practical joke on Melanie (pretending to believe
that Melanie is a sales clerk in a pet store) and Melanie plans
to return the "favor" by making a surprise delivery to Mitch
of the lovebirds he had been seeking for his younger sister,
both characters, well-groomed and stylishly dressed, seem
comfortable, capable, and confident. Both Mitch and Melanie
are treated deferentially by Mrs. MacGruder, the pet shop
clerk in the film's opening sequence; and after Mitch plays his
trick, Melanie, the daughter of a newspaper magnate, is able
to induce a reporter for her father's paper to access California
license-plate records in order to find out Mitch's identity. The
reporter may not be happy about it—at one point in the
conversation, Melanie says of the favor she is asking that,
"No, this is a small one," and later she playfully responds to

an unheard protest by the reporter by saying, "Pressure you? Why, Charlie, darling, would I try to pressure you?" —but he complies with her request.

When the film's action moves to Bodega Bay, both Mitch and Melanie find themselves constrained by the town's conservatism and traditionalism. Lee Edelman feels that Bodega Bay is "defined, as if allegorically, in opposition to San Francisco . . . [and] might stand for the concept of natural beauty."[28] Yet Bodega Bay is also what Philip Kolin refers to as a community "on the border, on the edge, between sea and land, continent and the vast deep; the quotidian and terror," located "at the very end of a respectable, putatively rational America."[29] It seems clear that Hitchcock chose Bodega Bay as a setting in part because of the town's ordinary qualities. As Robert A. Harris and Michael S. Lasky note, "The sleepy town of Bodega Bay where activity is slow and insignificant and people are involved in the trivial events of the day seems the most unlikely place for the wrath of the birds to be vented. Thus, when they do attack, it seems all the more vicious and malevolent."[30]

Cynthia Freeland points out the ordinary and work-a-day quality of Bodega Bay:

> Bodega Bay in this film is a run-down . . . fishing community, featuring no chic boutiques or yacht clubs. . . . It has family houses, an old-fashioned one-room school, a tiny post office and gas station, and one small restaurant that resembles a diner, complete with a resident alcoholic. Even the seemingly well-off Mrs. Brenner runs a poultry business, drives a truck, and worries about mundane matters of chicken feed.[31]

Bodega Bay certainly makes a different impression from San Francisco. With its "empty horizons," it "forms at best a pocket in the shore allied to the accident of commerce," an emphasis "echoed by the Spanish term *bodega*, a little market."[32]

Even before we first see Bodega Bay, we along with Melanie learn from one of Mitch's neighbors at Mitch's apartment building in San Francisco that Mitch leaves San

Figure 2. A foreign element enters a small town.

Francisco and makes the sixty-mile drive to Bodega Bay every weekend. Here Hitchcock may be using the film's two California settings to point out how we humans are not too different from the birds. As Scott Calef puts it, "Migration is [a] clear-cut case of instinctive behavior. But Mitch also 'migrates' as he commutes from San Francisco to Bodega Bay every weekend. A parallel is thus suggested between the habits of humans and birds."[33] Whereas Mitch migrates back and forth between big-city and small-town California, Melanie, whose own migratory pattern involves jet-setting back and forth between San Francisco and international destinations like Rome, does not know some parts of her own region very well. The extent to which Bodega Bay lies outside Melanie's sophisticated, modern, urban, San Francisco-based perspective becomes clear when Melanie responds to the neighbor's mention of Bodega Bay by saying, "Bodega Bay. Where's that?"

In *The Silent Scream: Alfred Hitchcock's Sound Track,* Elisabeth Weis suggests that Melanie's "intrusion into the peaceful hamlet of Bodega Bay is suggested predominantly by the noise of the sports car as she drives through the quiet streets."[34] Melanie's expensive British sports car, an Aston Martin DB-5, is literally foreign to Bodega Bay, just as the urbane and sophisticated Melanie is metaphorically foreign to the small fishing village (fig. 2). As Melanie speaks with the

Figure 3. The initially cautious but ultimately cordial store clerk.

townspeople of Bodega Bay, "Her lime green suit combines with other features of her self-presentation—her lipstick, nail varnish, fur coat, and gestures—to evoke a sense . . . of urban sophistication" that is "rather out of place in Bodega Bay."[35] The townspeople repeatedly express shock at Melanie's independence and her willingness to transcend traditional women's roles. When Melanie expresses her desire to rent a motorboat, the visibly surprised postmaster at the town post office asks, "You ever handle an outboard boat?" and a worker at the boatyard shakes his head in disbelief when Melanie arrives at the boatyard to take the boat out.

Robin Wood's impression of Bodega Bay is positive: "the small, easygoing little town [is] realized for us . . . through its general store with its associations of community life, friendliness, familiarity, security."[36] Yet the store is a crowded, claustrophobic place, with many examples of the kinds of cage images that will recur throughout the film. The disembodied voice of the storekeeper's colleague Harry comes in out of nowhere, as if the store is haunted. The initially cautious and guarded storekeeper turns out to be friendly and helpful (the wistful look he directs toward Melanie after she has gone [fig. 3], as if seeing her makes him wish he were a young man again, is a nice touch), but the information he and Harry give Melanie regarding the name of

Figure 4. The Bodega Bay waterfront, with the Brenner house far in the distance.

Mitch's younger sister (calling Cathy "Lois" or "Alice") is incorrect, contradicting the enduring image of the American small town as a place where, in contrast with the impersonality of the big city, everyone is supposed to know everyone else's name. As Kay Sloan puts it, "Melanie is a wild bird in a tradition-bound town," and in Bodega Bay "the society Melanie encounters . . . is a stifling one."[37]

As Richard Allen notes, while the spacious Brenner house, located "at the edge of Bodega bay," might seem to embody the California dream of the economic good life in a place of natural beauty and pleasant climate, it is nonetheless a place of "emotional distance and . . . isolation."[38] (fig. 4) The house is characterized by a dull color scheme in which drab browns predominate. Evidently, Hitchcock intended for the Brenner family to be part San Francisco, part Bodega Bay. In a preproduction meeting with Tippi Hedren, Hitchcock said of the character of Lydia that she "has a husband who was well off. He was probably director of a San Francisco corporation . . . and, after his death, left her reasonably comfortably off. I imagine they lived in San Francisco in an apartment and had this farm as a weekend place."[39]

In creating the Brenner farm, Hitchcock made sure that the art direction and set decoration for the location reproduced an actual Northern California locale with a strong sense of verisimilitude. As he told François Truffaut,

The house and farm we built ourselves. We made
an exact copy of the existing houses. There was an
old Russian farm built around 1849. There were
many Russians living on the coast at that time, and
there's even a town called Sebastopol some twelve
miles northeast of Bodega Bay. When the Russians
owned Alaska, they used to come down the coast to
hunt seals.[40]

In this case, Hitchcock's concern for accuracy of detail was
matched by a determination to use setting to reinforce the
film's tone, particularly with regard to the emotionally cold
qualities of the Brenner home as it is presented in the film. As
Richard Allen puts it, "the Brenner household, in particular
the family's living room, is a space denuded of color and lit by
black lampshades (in a living room!), articulating the sense of
emotional desiccation and emptiness that is attached to the
character of Lydia Brenner after the death of her husband."[41]

The same qualities of emotional coldness that characterize
the Brenner home also apply to the home of Annie Hayworth
(Suzanne Pleshette), whose relationship with Mitch was
thwarted by Lydia's opposition, and who has remained in
Bodega Bay as a schoolteacher because she wants to hold on
to Mitch's friendship. Hitchcock seems to have wanted Annie
Hayworth to bridge the two California worlds of San
Francisco and Bodega Bay. Hitchcock told Truffaut that

The home of the schoolteacher is a combination of a
schoolteacher's house in San Francisco and the home
of a schoolteacher in Bodega Bay. I covered it both
ways because, as you may remember, the
schoolteacher in that picture works in Bodega Bay but
she comes from San Francisco.[42]

Strangely, however, Annie's house seems to be a combination
of the worst of both worlds. The home is full of books that she
is never shown reading; and the recording of Richard
Wagner's *Tristan und Isolde* (an operatic retelling of a tragic

medieval story of forbidden love) both demonstrates the high level of education and cultural sophistication that Annie never gets to put to actual use in Bodega Bay and shows that she has never really gotten over her thwarted love for Mitch.

A later dialogue between Melanie and Cathy likewise draws attention to the differences between Bodega Bay and San Francisco, as well as reinforcing the emphasis that Evan Hunter's script places on questions of community identification, as Cathy tries to persuade Melanie to attend her upcoming surprise birthday party. The divide between city and country seems to receive special emphasis here; there is an emotional edge to the way Cathy asks, "Don't you like Bodega Bay?" and Cathy seems disappointed when Melanie replies, "I don't know yet." Cathy seems anxious to champion the country against the city, saying that "Mitch likes it very much" and adding that he says "San Francisco's like an anthill at the foot of a bridge." Melanie's reply—"Oh, I suppose it does get a little hectic at times"—seems reserved, as if to imply that, regardless, she feels much more at home in San Francisco than she ever could in Bodega Bay.

Mitch too brings up the links and divides between San Francisco and Bodega Bay when he bids Melanie good night after the dinner. When he asks if he can see her again, Melanie replies, "San Francisco's a long way from here," a remark that can be taken metaphorically as well as literally. Mitch replies, "Well, I'm in San Francisco five days a week with a lot of time on my hands." Perhaps Mitch, the urbane and successful San Francisco lawyer, still has a bit of small-town intolerance in him: this dialogue, which follows a kitchen conversation in which Lydia has made clear her disapproval of Melanie, suddenly takes a nasty turn, as Mitch treats Melanie with a cruelty that had been lacking in his previous practical joke against her in the bird shop.

Invoking newspaper reports that Melanie had jumped naked into a fountain in Rome—what Richard Allen terms "an unusually explicit reference to Italian Cinema" and more specifically to "Anita Ekberg's exploits in the Trevi Fountain in *La Dolce Vita*"[43]—Mitch suggests that they could go swimming together and says with a smirk, "Yeah, I'd really like to swim. I think we could get along very well." Melanie rejects Mitch's sarcastic remarks with indignation; but because she is not in her usual place, among the members of her customary social circle, she cannot do so with her usual self-assurance. In a preproduction meeting with Hedren, Hitchcock said regarding this sequence that

> Had [Melanie] been among San Franciscans, you know, and somebody from [suburban] Burlingame . . . some guy from Burlingame had made that crack, she'd have just . . . turned her back on him and said . . . `The hell with it.' I think she's already been attracted to the young man, and there's a kind of a bit of a disappointment that she finds, because she's beginning to get interested in these sort of people, you see, as a fresh thing that she's come across, and I think that there's a general sobering up here.[44]

When Melanie returns to Annie's house, her education in the ways of Bodega Bay continues. Offering Melanie a sweater or quilt, Annie almost seems to be speaking the language of the travel guide when she says, "It gets a bit chilly here at night, especially if you're over near the bay." It becomes clear that Annie, originally a San Franciscan, has come to identify with Bodega Bay over her four years of living there, asking Melanie, "So, how do you like *our* little hamlet?" (emphasis added). When Melanie, still angry that the dinner at the Brenner farm did not turn out well, says, "I despise it," Annie smiles and replies, "Well, I suppose it doesn't offer much to the casual visitor, unless you're thrilled by a collection of shacks on a hillside" — a remark that recalls the earlier reference to San Francisco as an anthill at the foot of a bridge. While the big city of San Francisco and the small country town of Bodega Bay have many significant and readily detectable differences, they are both places where, beneath a surface of apparent safety, human beings are vulnerable to malice and harm.

Induced by an apologetic phone call from Mitch to reconsider her earlier plans to return at once to San Francisco, Melanie attends Kathy's surprise birthday party the following day. During the early stages of the party, Mitch and Melanie converse on a hill above the home where the party is taking place, and Melanie again emphasizes her ties to San Francisco. When Mitch asks, "Why do you have to rush off? What's so important in San Francisco?" Melanie replies, "On Tuesdays, I take a course in General Semantics at Berkeley," mentioning the university that is preeminent among the San Francisco area's public institutions of higher learning. Moreover, as John Hellmann suggests, "Melanie's enrollment in the course at Berkeley . . . also suggests that Hitchcock's protagonist is interested in the alternative ways of thinking and living being developed in the California of the early sixties."[45] While California could be a decidedly conservative bastion of American aspirations for material prosperity within a shared set of social and cultural expectations—the sort of cultural landscape that gave rise to the John Birch Society—it could also provide, in Berkeley, "a signifier in public consciousness for . . . leftist agitation that voiced a radical dissent from the political and social taboos constraining Cold War politics and culture," the kind of sociological landscape in which even an affluent young woman like Melanie Daniels could be "exposed to poetry readings and political dissent at the coffee houses and clubs adjacent to the campus."[46]

Exhibiting a degree of social consciousness that had not been apparent before, Melanie describes raising money for the education of a Korean child (the long-term devastation of the Korean War would have been as apparent for the people of that time as the lasting impact of the Iraq War is for us), and mentions that she works for Travelers' Aid at San Francisco International Airport. This conversation is also where Melanie for the first time reveals the pained reality behind her carefree party-girl façade, confiding that she felt "lost" among her pleasure-seeking friends in Rome, and that she now tries to fill her life with more meaningful activities. Most crucially, Melanie admits to the underlying source of her pain, telling

Mitch that her mother "ran off with a hotel man from the East," and abandoned San Francisco and the Daniels family's affluent way of life for reasons unknown.

This conversation between Melanie and Mitch is interrupted by a bird attack on the young girls at the surprise party, which leaves the children with a few cuts and an unknown degree of emotional trauma but no fatalities. The first fatality of the Bodega Bay bird attacks comes later: Lydia goes to the nearby Fawcett farm and finds the home devastated by another bird attack—windows broken, teacups smashed—and Dan Fawcett lying dead and bloody on the floor of his bedroom, his eyes pecked out. Hitchcock's presentation of that rural scene, particularly in the sequence when Lydia is driving out to the Fawcett farm on a quiet dirt road amid green farm fields, with the only sound being the quiet hum of the truck motor, has much in common with how he presents Bodega Bay generally: "that wonderfully evocative and disturbing landscape: calm-seeming, yet ominous in its stillness; beautiful, yet somber beneath the dullish sky."[47] Small wonder, perhaps, that in a scene that was written for the movie but never filmed, Melanie, talking with Mitch while Lydia is off at Dan Fawcett's farm, tells Mitch, "I'm frightened and confused and I . . . I think I want to go back to San Francisco where there are buildings and . . . and concrete and . . . everything I know."[48] But for Melanie, there is no going back to San Francisco: she is stuck in Bodega Bay, a community whose social fault lines are about to become only too apparent.

Social Breakdown at the Tides Restaurant

Hitchcock's examination of the divisions within an ostensibly unified California (and, by implication, U.S.) society in *The Birds* takes on greatest clarity in the sequence set in the Tides Restaurant shortly after a bird attack on the Bodega Bay School—a sequence so complete and self-contained that it could work as a one-act play. In the restaurant, as John P. McCombe points out, the "orderly rows of bottles behind the bar [constitute a] conscious choice in the *mise-en-scène* that suggests humanity's futile attempt to impose order on the surrounding world."[49] For Christopher Sharrett, the people inside the restaurant constitute "a microcosm of society."[50] Evan Hunter had written to Hitchcock that "You will find in this scene an alarmist, a pacifist, and various other types," and the diversity in background among the people in the diner reflects the variety of opinions within the Bodega Bay community regarding how to explain and address the problem of the bird attacks.[51]

Hunter's reference to "various other types" shows how the screenwriter worked to make sure that the people at the Tides Inn are types, "representatives of small-town, middle America," rather than fully individuated characters.[52] Ian Cameron and Richard Jeffrey note that through the Bodega Bay citizenry assembled in the Tides Restaurant, Hitchcock as director and Hunter as screenwriter focus upon

> the attitude of comfortably civilized people towards nature. The people of Bodega Bay do what the rugged pioneers could not; they represent *us*. . . . Their attitudes are very typical and, furthermore, we are made to find ourselves sharing them. They could mostly be summed up by one complacent answer to the question, what is nature there for? It is there for us.[53]

As a prelude to the scene's setting forth of citizens' discordant reactions to a crisis situation, Melanie offers firsthand testimony regarding the bird attack she just witnessed. Deke, the owner of the restaurant, seems willing to believe Melanie's explanation that the attack was unprovoked. Others in the diner, however, refuse to see the bird attacks in any context outside their area of familiarity and expertise. Indeed, as Bernard F. Dick says, "the residents of Bodega Bay . . . are as insular in their thinking as du Maurier's islanders were in the original."[54] The town drunk—who speaks with an Irish accent that may represent the limits of cultural diversity in monolithically white Bodega Bay, and whose presence in the restaurant may represent a redoubled reference to Sean

O'Casey's plays about social disintegration—quotes phrases from the Bible and insists repeatedly that "It's the end of the world." Mitch, a lawyer whose profession relates to the maintenance of the social order, seeks practical ways of protecting the town against the bird attacks—"We'll make our own fog. We'll use smokepots, the way the army does"—and solicits the help of leading townspeople.

One of those leading townspeople is Sebastian Sholes, a fishing-boat captain and business leader of the community, whose captain's hat indicates his occupational and leadership status. Sholes mentions that seagulls swarmed one of his boats—"Playing devil with my fishing boats. . . . A whole flock of gulls nearly capsized one of my boats—nearly tore the skipper's arm off"—but is reluctant to commit himself publicly to any course of action regarding the bird attacks, "even if this is true." In an odd *non sequitur*, Sholes responds to Mitch's appeals for help by saying, "I like Bodega Bay as well as the next man, but . . ." The ellipsis speaks to an unstated premise: that Sholes, who has always been willing to take on the responsibilities of leadership within the parameters of the possible as he has understood them all his life, is unwilling to act, even to protect his community, when something radically new and outside those parameters endangers that community.

Christopher Sharrett suggests that "Mitch's integration in the community has the effect of disturbing it; as a well-to-do lawyer his presence suggests the 'gentrification' of the town and the disruption of the simple values of a working class settlement."[55] My own reading is somewhat different. Mitch's weekly returns to Bodega Bay do not seem to make him a threat to the people of Bodega Bay; indeed, his former fellow-townspeople consistently treat him with the same respect that he, an eminent citizen by virtue of his education and professional achievements, consistently shows to all, without a trace of condescension. Sholes seems to respect Mitch's ideas as much as everyone else does. Yet concerned perhaps that taking a stand of some kind might result in some diminution of his own prestige within the community, Sholes refuses to act, in spite of Mitch's insistence that "You're an important man in this town. If you help, they all will." Even Mitch's invocation of the factuality of the situation—"It's happening, isn't it?"—will not stir Sholes from his apathy. He says, with regard to the question of believing that the bird attacks are occurring, "Frankly, I don't"—literally distrusting his own senses.

Mrs. Bundy, an amateur ornithologist whose beret bespeaks her status as a self-proclaimed intellectual—and who perhaps provides an affectionate parody of source author Daphne du Maurier, a well-known polymath—plays the rational expert, saying, "Let's be logical about this." She rattles off statistics and factoids regarding the number of birds in the world, the first bird (*Archaeopteryx*), the sizes of birds' brainpans, and so forth, and on that basis alone rejects Melanie's eyewitness testimony, stating that the very concept of birds of different species flocking together is "unimaginable." In a manner showing that her attitude toward birds is romantic dilettantism rather than the realistic perspective of a professional scientist, she adds, "Birds are not aggressive creatures, miss. They bring beauty to the world." Mrs. Bundy follows this declaration with what could be a reference to environmental degradation or to fears of a nuclear conflict, saying, "It is mankind, rather, who insists upon making it difficult for life to exist upon this planet." "Poor things," Mrs. Bundy later says of seagulls that reportedly got lost in the fog at Santa Cruz and crashed into buildings, though she expresses no comparable concern for human children who were just attacked in her own town. Like Sholes, Mrs. Bundy literally cannot think outside her frame of reference. Because her ornithological textbooks and monographs teach her that birds of different species cannot act in concert, she is capable of ignoring the evidence of her own senses.

Like Captain Sholes and Mrs. Bundy, other people in the diner demonstrate similar limitations in their thinking. Those limitations reflect the social roles that these characters accept as defining their personality and being, roles that they are unwilling to try to transcend A fedora-wearing businessman meanwhile expresses his hatred for all birds and his belief that they should all be killed: "Get yourself guns and wipe them off the face of the earth! . . . Kill 'em all. Get rid of 'em. Messy things." His anger seems disproportionate to the situation at hand, more like what a Cold Warrior of the time might have said about the Soviets, or like what any militarist of any era might say regarding an "other" that he (usually he) has determined is an implacable enemy deserving of extermination. Malone, the small-town deputy, seems willing to believe whatever other police officers from a bigger city might tell him to believe, saying of the killing of Dan Fawcett that "Santa Rosa police think it's a felony murder." And a mother of two young children who has stopped at the restaurant on her way back to San Francisco perhaps displaces her own fear onto her offspring—"Could you ask them to lower their voices, please? They're frightening the children"—though she does express incredulity at the unwillingness of most of the Bodega Bay residents to believe Melanie. It may be noteworthy in that regard that the mother is a big-city outsider, a San Franciscan, like Melanie, Annie (formerly), and Mitch (five days a week).

The in-depth conversation among all these people constitutes "a contemporary Tower of Babel," as Neil P. Hurley terms it.[56] And just as that chaotic, multilingual conversation in the Old Testament prevented the tower from being built, so all that talking in the Tides Restaurant does nothing to effectively respond to a subsequent large-scale bird attack on the town, in which the businessman who had expressed an irrational hatred for all birds is the first to die. Moreover, the death of the businessman underscores what Harris and Lasky see as "One of the themes that [pervade] the entire story . . . the failure of communication"; Melanie and the other people still inside the diner "all scream at him not to drop the match, but in their garbled unison entreaty he cannot understand them and drops the match, causing a fiery explosion."[57] Throughout the entire scene, the viewer senses the frustration that Mitch and Melanie feel as the other people in the diner fail to see a crisis situation outside of their frames of reference: conservative, sensible, business-oriented community leadership for Sholes; existing scientific knowledge for Mrs. Bundy; a "common sense"-based law-enforcement community consensus for Deputy Malone; a casual, thoughtless appeal to mass violence by the businessman; and, for the mother visiting from San Francisco, the instinct to protect the young. It is no surprise, then, that after a demonstration of their limited understanding and inability to communicate with each other, the people in the diner cannot convey a coherent message of warning to a man whose life is in danger.

As the bird attack unfolds—the first truly large-scale and public attack in the film, and the first to target the heart of the town as opposed to outlying areas such as a farm or a home or a school—the diner and "the town centre [become] the locale of panic and disintegration," as Raymond Durgnat puts it.[58] Tom Cohen sees significance in the fact that during the attack, Melanie takes shelter in a telephone booth, a communications center from which she can send no communications that will help anyone else or secure any help for her, while the birds "attack *telephone booths* and would disrupt imprinting."[59] Perhaps it is because of the failures of communication symbolized by an inoperatve telephone booth that David Sterritt feels that *The Birds* "is *about* the futility of language. The more its characters talk among themselves, the more extreme their problems become. By contrast, birds cannot talk, write, or use language in any way that a human could identify; yet they seem ever more organized and unified in the narrative."[60] This sequence seems to focus especially on the idea that the people of the small town where everyone supposedly knows everyone can do no more to communicate meaningfully and respond to crisis than can the anonymous, alienated masses of the large city.

Camille Paglia calls attention to the manner in which, during the bird attack, "civilisation collapses in Bodega Bay— with the police and fire companies helpless and an incongruous, horse-drawn wagon stampeding out of the wild West."[61] The last of these details is particularly significant. The horse-drawn wagon is too *outré* a detail for a director as detail-conscious as Hitchcock to have included by accident. Nor is the timing of this shot coincidental: we see the horse-

Figure 5. The birds'-eye view of Bodega Bay under attack.

drawn wagon right after the attacking birds have destroyed the town's gasoline station, thereby cutting off the fuel supply for Bodega Bay motorists. In the visual spectacle of the gasoline station's destruction—Martyn Shawcross reports that du Maurier "was more than pleased with the results" of Hitchcock's adaptation of her work, and particularly liked the attack on the Bodega Bay gas station[62]—Hitchcock seems to be drawing attention to the widely held belief of the time that nuclear war would result in a backward movement of civilization. One thinks here of Albert Einstein's frequently quoted remark when asked how World War III would be fought: "I do not know how the Third World War will be fought, but I can tell you what they will use in the Fourth— rocks."[63] The arrangement of these shots seems meant to indicate that a traumatic crisis like the bird attacks can quickly have the effect of moving a society away from its modern "civilized" comforts and back towards barbarism.

The famous shot from above as the attack unfolds, with the camera taking a literal bird's-eye view of the chaos in the streets and the fire from the burning gasoline pump, forces the viewer to distance himself or herself from the human suffering on the ground, and from the comforting illusion that the American small town is characterized by an emotional closeness missing in the big city (fig. 5). From the birds' point of view, Bodega Bay and San Francisco might look remarkably alike. Moreover, this shot forces the viewer to take on the perspective of the attacking birds, the monstrous force threatening the lives of the people of Bodega Bay. In the process, Hitchcock engages in part of his ongoing reflection regarding the nature of the monstrous. Slavoj Žižek defines Hitchcock's filmic monsters as

> machines which run blindly, without compassion . . . inaccessible to our pleas . . . yet at the same time they are defined by the presence of an absolute gaze. What is truly horrifying about a monster is the way it seems to watch us all the time—without this gaze, the blind insistence of its drive would lose its uncanny character and turn into a simple mechanical force.[64]

The blind destructive drive of the birds—they do not seem to be targeting humans as a food source, or to be defending their young—is linked with the blindness images and references that occur throughout the film: the pecked-out eyes of Dan Fawcett at the Fawcett farm; Mitch shouting "Cover your faces! Cover your eyes!" during the birds' first attack on the Brenner farmhouse; the broken eyeglasses of a girl chased by the birds during the attack on the school; the manner in which Melanie, during the birds' final attack against her in an upstairs room of the Brenner farmhouse, uses a flashlight to fend off a gull just as it is about to attack her eyes. Susan Smith links these blindness images with the way in which various characters in the film habitually say "I see" to indicate self-assurance based on their knowledge of the reality of their situation; as Smith puts it, the characters' "confident claims of being able to 'see' during the initial phase of the narrative are undermined in the most fundamental, brutal way possible by the birds' specific targeting of the eyes during the attacks."[65]

When the attack has ended, we see further evidence of the mindset of this small California town. A group of women who have taken shelter in a hallway of the diner eye Melanie suspiciously. A broken-looking Mrs. Bundy huddles in a seat in the hallway, her rationalist confidence gone. Especially important in this scene is the mother from San Francisco, who seems to have adopted the small town's distrust of outsiders with remarkable speed and readiness. Margaret Horwitz characterizes the mother as an embodiment of "female hysteria" and points out parallels between her and Lydia: "Like Lydia she has two children, a boy and a girl, and no husband, and she holds her children under her arms (wings) like a mother hen."[66] While Mitch looks on uneasily, the mother walks up to Melanie and says, "They say when you got here this whole thing started. Who are you? What are you? Where did you come from? I think you're the cause of all this. I think you're evil! Evil!" As in Don Siegel's science-fiction film *Invasion of the Body Snatchers* (1956), a seemingly idyllic California community becomes a site for the enactment of small-town American paranoia toward and distrust of outsiders, a locale for the dehumanization of a perceived "other."

The women—"birds," in the parlance of Hitchcock's British homeland—have found in Melanie a scapegoat they can jointly accuse. There may not be a deliberate allusion to the Harpies from Greek mythology and their tormenting of the blind prophet Phineas, but one does think of the popular use of the word to describe a group of women using the advantage of numbers to act cruelly and aggressively. Actress Doreen Lang, who plays the mother (the credits officially refer to her as "Hysterical Mother in Diner") had played the same sort of character before. In *The Wrong Man* (1956) she played Ann James, an insurance company employee who wrongly identifies musician Manny Balestrero (Henry Fonda) as the one who robbed them. The irrational manner in which Lang's character in *The Wrong Man* continues to insist on Balestrero's guilt, even in the face of overwhelming evidence of his innocence, looks ahead to the unreasonable way in which Lang as the mother in the Tides Restaurant blames a catastrophic bird attack on a single human being. In both instances, others seem to share the Lang character's beliefs, and Hitchcock thus emphasizes how irrational beliefs can spread quickly, like a contagion.

Figure 6. The hysterical mother confronts Melanie and
the spectators of the film.

It is also noteworthy that "The accusations of the
hysterical mother in the diner" are, as Ryan Halwani and
Steven Jones note, "underscored by their direct delivery to the
camera."[67] Through Hitchcock's use of subjective camera, we,
like Melanie, are directly targeted by the mother's accusations
(fig. 6), just as moments before the viewer was "directly
targeted" by birds that flew straight toward the camera as
they struck the telephone booth in which Melanie was
trapped. Like Melanie, most viewers of *The Birds* would be,
through the medium of cinema, "first-time visitors" to
Bodega Bay, California, bringing with them a different social
and cultural background from that of the people of the small
fishing-based coastal town. And, like Melanie, the viewer
might find him- or herself feeling vulnerable to the mother's
charges. After all, the mother is quite right in asserting that
the bird attacks did not begin until an outsider (Melanie, as
well as those other visitors, the spectators of the film) showed
up in Bodega Bay.

Like Melanie, we are likely to feel that the mother's
charges against Melanie, or against us, are unjustified—an
ideological position that further distances us from the film's
Bodega Bay and its people, while offering a critique of the
fearful American society of the nuclear-era 1960's. Indeed,
Peter Conrad feels that the various people in the diner "are

present in Hitchcock's film in order to suggest that there may be reasons for expunging the malign, brawling race to which they belong," and that the diner scene "exists to prompt Hitchcock's misanthropic view on humanity."[68] Yet Conrad's singularly bleak interpretation of Hitchcock's world-view as expressed in *The Birds* leaves a great many things out. One thinks of the sympathetic qualities of the film's major characters. Melanie Daniels may act like a dilettante at times, but she has endured depths of emotional anguish and abandonment, and she shows courage, resourcefulness, and concern for others. Mitch can be smug, judgmental, and full of himself; but he also shows compassion, understanding, and a willingness to admit when he is wrong. Annie Hayworth would theoretically have every reason to be envious of Melanie, yet she offers Melanie hospitality, honest conversation, and sound advice. Lydia, for all her hostility toward Melanie, displays a willingness to speak honestly with Melanie about her fears and concerns. Cathy, with all her emotional neediness, wants not only to be loved but to give love as well. The Tides Restaurant sequence portrays a diverse group of people whose varying degrees and varieties of closed-mindedness make them generally unsympathetic. Yet because of the care with which Hitchcock has set forth the sympathetic qualities of characters like Melanie, Mitch, Annie, Lydia, and Cathy, an alert viewer will take from this story a sense that human communities can survive the challenges of crisis situations. That happy outcome, however, is not inevitable; there must be a core group of ethically aware individuals, people who can look beyond the limitations of their own socially constructed perspectives, if human societies are to survive the challenges they face.

Survival—For the Individual and the Community

The question of who will or will not survive is a traditional trope of the apocalypse narrative and disaster movies—a dramatization of the idea that survival in a crisis situation may be a matter of chance, or may be a function of the choices one makes. When Mitch and Melanie go to Annie's house to get Cathy, only to learn that yet another bird attack occurred at the house, Cathy relates the sad details: a large group of birds attacked suddenly and without warning, and Annie pushed Cathy inside the house just before the birds covered and killed Annie. In the wake of Annie's self-sacrifice, the viewer sees just how much the once-carefree Melanie has grown and developed. As Michael Walker points out, "It is Melanie who is the guiding intelligence here: who first thinks of Cathy, who stops Mitch from angrily throwing a stone at the crows, who tells him not to leave Annie's body outside."[69] Perhaps Hitchcock is suggesting that both Melanie and Mitch, these two characters from backgrounds of wealth and privilege who have enjoyed life without taking it too seriously, have grown in dignity and knowledge as a result of the ordeal they are enduring together.

The idea that individuals like Mitch and Melanie can respond to crisis by growing and developing in positive ways, even as the community around them seems to be devolving, is reemphasized when Mitch and Melanie board up the windows of the Brenner farmhouse, preparing for the next bird attack in a way that recalls white settlers of the West fortifying their frontier homes against attacks by hostile Native Americans. Looking at Bodega Bay from the rooftop, Mitch says to Melanie, "Doesn't look so very different, does it? A little smoke hanging over the town—but otherwise, not that different." With Mitch's words, we get a sense that Bodega Bay has all but ceased to exist as an organized human community. About all we can infer is that other citizens of Bodega Bay are doing as Mitch, Melanie, Lydia, and Annie are doing—reconfiguring their homes as cages in which they will deliberately imprison themselves while animals roam free outside, reversing the customary order. Seeing birds heading inland, Melanie and Mitch muse aloud about where the birds might be heading. "Santa Rosa?" Melanie asks. "Maybe," Mitch replies—and the alert viewer of Hitchcock's work might at once detect an allusion to the moment in *Shadow of a Doubt* when sunny Santa Rosa revealed its dark side.

When the members of a community face crisis, and all that they can see is the trauma inflicted by that crisis, they may look to more powerful outside authorities for assurance that the larger social order still holds. In that context, it is more than understandable that the characters trapped in the Brenner house do likewise. A news announcer, identified as a San Francisco journalist by Lydia, announces in a smoothly professional voice that

> In Bodega Bay early this morning, a large flock of crows attacked a group of children who were leaving the school during a fire drill. One little girl was seriously injured and taken to the hospital in Santa Rosa, but the majority of children reached safety. We understand there was another attack on the town, but this information is rather sketchy. So far, no word has come through to show if there have been further attacks.

Mitch's response to the radio report is a frustrated "Well, is that all?" expressing his sense that there is no help, not even any useful information, coming in from the outside. As with du Maurier's source story, wherein the British protagonist finds the B.B.C.'s radio reports on the bird attacks to be of no use in the situation that he and the people he loves are facing, so the reports from the San Francisco news station have no real relevance to the survival situation faced by Mitch, Melanie, Lydia, and Cathy.

The radio broadcast, with its vague and far-from-hopeful generalities, fails utterly as a source of comfort, hope, new information, or even practical tips by which the people of the communities being attacked by the birds might survive. As a result, the thematic idea that Mitch, Melanie, Lydia, and Cathy can rely only upon their own inner resources of courage and resourcefulness receives further emphasis. Later, while preparing for the group's final flight away from Bodega Bay, to try to get the badly injured Melanie to a hospital in San Francisco, Mitch listens to a car radio broadcast that provides one final bit of worrisome information: "The bird attacks have subsided for the time being. Bodega Bay appears to be the center, though there are reports of minor attacks on Sebastopol and a few on Santa Rosa." The radio broadcast seems noteworthy for the way it sets forth another nuclear-era parallel: the bird attacks seem to be spreading from an epicenter, like fallout from a nuclear bomb, with bird attacks "radiating out" from Bodega Bay to Sebastopol (fourteen miles northeast of Bodega Bay) and then beyond that to Santa Rosa (seven miles northeast of Sebastopol). How much farther might the bird attacks go? The answer, to incorporate some of the radio announcer's final words from the broadcast, "does not seem clear as yet."

The uncertainty and lack of resolution of the film's conclusion, as Mitch, Melanie, Lydia, and Cathy drive away from the Brenner farm in Melanie's sports car, stand in contrast with other concluding ideas that Hitchcock had considered. He told Peter Bogdanovich that "For the ordinary public—they [Mitch, Melanie, Cathy, and Lydia] got away to San Francisco—but I toyed with the idea of lap-dissolving on them in the car, looking, and there is the Golden Gate Bridge—covered in birds."[70] It is interesting to contemplate Hitchcock setting forth such a dire fate for his beloved San Francisco; ultimately, it seems, he preferred to conclude the film on a more ambiguous note.

Driving Away from Bodega Bay

I have screened *The Birds* in many film classes at various colleges and universities, and I have found that my students consistently focus on two features of the film's concluding passages. The first is that the electronically generated bird sounds seem to get louder as the film moves toward its conclusion (it is interesting that the last bird we see is the raven that briefly nipped at Mitch's hand—perhaps an allusion to one of Hitchcock's favorite writers, Edgar Allan Poe). The second is the ray of light that shines down from the clouds toward the point on the horizon toward which Mitch, Cathy, Lydia, and Melanie are driving. These visual and auditory cues, which at first might seem to contradict each other, call to mind Robin Wood's assertion that "the degree of optimism or pessimism it [the conclusion] is felt to contain must depend on ourselves"—because "life is a matter of beating off the birds, and the only (partial) security is in the formation of deep relationships."[71] The emphasis in the concluding shots does seem to be on the idea that these characters have, at least for the moment, survived as a kind of reconstituted, postmodern family. Lydia's hostility toward Melanie is a thing of the past, and they are moving forward together. Yet the range of critical commentary that the film's conclusion has encouraged, including arguments that would characterize the conclusion less optimistically than I have, indicates that Hitchcock wanted to end his film on a note that emphasized ambiguity.

The ambiguity of Alfred Hitchcock's portrayal of California society in *The Birds* reflects what other writers and thinkers have said about life in the Golden State. For instance, Dora Beale Polk concludes her study *The Island of California,* a history of the centuries-old vision of California as mythic paradise, by suggesting that the latest manifestation of the long-cherished California dream is

> A nightmare, we might rather say. For it is not an ideal island of gold, pearls, and liberated women that [some] have in mind, but an apocalypse of annihilation. Enraptured by such fantasies, some predict that California will break off into the ocean at the next great earthquake. Others envision it as collapsing under the weight of the millions crowding across her borders seeking the gold of her sun, her commerce, her groves, her beaches, her thousand golden hills.[72]

Clearly, Hitchcock, filming at a time of widespread cultural anxiety regarding the prospects of nuclear war, had a different sort of potential apocalypse in mind. He once claimed that "the theme of *The Birds* is don't mess about or tamper with nature. Look, man's fooled around with uranium 235 out of the ground and look where it's brought us."[73] Similarly, Hitchcock told an interviewer for *Cinema* that "*The Birds* expresses nature and what it can do, and the dangers of nature, because there is no doubt if the birds did decide, you know, with the millions that there are, to go for everybody's eyes, then we'd have H.G. Wells' Kingdom of the Blind on our hands."[74] Yet beyond the director's expressed general anxieties regarding a world gone science-mad without fear of consequences, the California society of *The Birds* more specifically reflects what the British-born Hitchcock found problematic regarding the insular outlook of his film's Bodega Bay, of California, and, by implication, of American society generally.

Examples of the selfless, other-centered *individual*—Annie Hayworth, and, as the film goes on, Melanie Daniels and Mitch Brenner—are contrasted with the far more numerous rugged American *individualists* of Bodega Bay, California, who talk a great deal in order to vindicate their own opinions but do nothing meaningful to help preserve their community in the face of a shared threat to all. Given that reality of the imperfections, tensions, and social fissures that exist in every community, *The Birds* offers what may be Hitchcock's most profound reflection on the importance and ability of human beings forming meaningful relationships with each other. When a crisis situation occurs, there will often be people who are unable to respond to that crisis outside the restrictions of their prejudices, their preconceptions, their frames of reference—people like most of the participants in that conversation at the Tides Restaurant. Such people may not be of much help in the face of a danger that is truly new and unfamiliar. We might do better, when crisis occurs, to trust in people like Melanie, Mitch, Annie, Lydia, and Cathy—people who are willing to question the norms of their world, to acknowledge their own faults, to think in new ways and develop new ideas in response to new problems—to meet a crisis and achieve a restoration of the good. It may seem a limited hope, but it is probably the best hope we have.

Notes

1. Alfred Hitchcock, "It's a Bird, It's a Plane, It's . . . *The Birds*," *Hitchcock on Hitchcock: Selected Writings and Interviews*, ed. Sidney Gottlieb (Berkeley and Los Angeles: University of California Press, 1995), 315.

2. John Russell Taylor, *Hitch: The Life and Times of Alfred Hitchcock* (New York: Pantheon Books, 1978), 268.

3. Donald Spoto, *The Art of Alfred Hitchcock: Fifty Years of His Motion Pictures* (New York: Anchor Books, 1992), 330.

4. Kevin Starr, *California: A History* (New York: Modern Library, 2007), 343.

5. Joan Didion, *Slouching Towards Bethlehem* (New York: Farrar, Straus and Giroux, 1990), 172.

6. William Rothman, *Hitchcock—The Murderous Gaze* (Cambridge, Massachusetts: Harvard University Press, 1982), 249.

7. Neil P. Hurley, *Soul in Suspense: Hitchcock's Fright and Delight* (Metuchen, New Jersey: Scarecrow Press, 1993), 210.

8. Bernard F. Dick, "Hitchcock's Terrible Mothers," *Literature/Film Quarterly* 28, no. 4 (2000): 243.

9. Jonathan Freedman and Richard H. Millington, "Introduction," in *Hitchcock's America*, eds. Jonathan Freedman and Richard Millington (New York: Oxford University Press, 1999), 5.

10. Cynthia Freeland, "Natural Evil in the Horror Film: Alfred Hitchcock's *The Birds*," in *The Changing Face of Evil in the Horror Film*, ed. Martin F. Norden (Amsterdam: Rodopi, 2007), 59.

11. Irving Singer, *Three Philosophical Filmmakers: Hitchcock, Welles, Renoir* (Cambridge: Massachusetts Institute of Technology Press, 2004), 56.

12. Joel W. Finler, *Hitchcock in Hollywood* (New York: Continuum Publishing, 1992), 138.

13. Ian Cameron and V.F. Perkins, "Hitchcock," in *Alfred Hitchcock: Interviews*, ed. Sidney Gottlieb (Jackson: University Press of Mississippi, 2003), 49.

14. American Film Institute, "Dialogue on Film: Alfred Hitchcock," in *Alfred Hitchcock: Interviews*, 100.

15. Peter Bogdanovich, *The Cinema of Alfred Hitchcock* (New York: Museum of Modern Art, 1963), 44.

16. Kyle B. Counts, "The Making of Alfred Hitchcock's *The Birds*: The Complete Story Behind the Precursor of Modern Horror Films," *Cinefantastique* 10 (fall 1980): 16.

17. Counts, "The Making of Alfred Hitchcock's *The Birds*," 17.

18. Robert E. Kapsis, "Hollywood Filmmaking and Reputation Building: Hitchcock's *The Birds*," *Journal of Popular Film & Television* 15, no. 1 (spring 1987): 6-7.

19. Howard Maxford, *The A-Z of Hitchcock* (London: B.T. Batsford, 2002), 45.

20. John Orr, *Hitchcock and Twentieth-Century Cinema* (London: Wallflower Press, 2005), 72-73.

21. Richard Allen, "Hitchcock and the Wandering Woman: The Influence of Italian Art Cinema on *The Birds*," *Hitchcock Annual* 13 (2013), 151.

22. Charlotte Chandler, *It's Only a Movie: Alfred Hitchcock—A Personal Biography* (New York: Simon and Schuster, 2005), 238.

23. Matthew Richard Poole and Erika Lenkert, *Frommer's San Francisco 2009* (Hoboken, New Jersey: Wiley Publishing, 2008), 56.

24. Alan Tucker, gen. ed., *The Penguin Guide to San Francisco and Northern California 1991* (New York: Penguin Books, 1991), 28.

25. Ken Mogg, "Will and Wilfulness: Recent Commentary on Hitchcock's *The Birds*," *Screening the Past* 12, online at www.latrobe.edu.au/www/screeningthepast/firstrelease/fr0301/kmfr12a.htm.

26. Tom Cohen, *Hitchcock's Cryptonymies, Volume II: War Machines* (Minneapolis: University of Minnesota Press, 2005), 153.

27. Peter Conrad, *The Hitchcock Murders* (London: Faber and Faber, 2000), 274. "Hoardings" is a British term for billboards.

28. Lee Edelman, "Hitchcock's Future," in *Alfred Hitchcock: Centenary Essays*, eds. Richard Allen and Sam Ishii-Gonzalès (London: British Film Institute, 1999), 247.

29. Philip C. Kolin, "'A Play About Terrible Birds': Tennessee Williams's *The Gnädiges Fraulein* and Alfred Hitchcock's *The Birds*," *South Atlantic Review* 66, no. 1 (winter 2001): 16.

30. Robert A. Harris and Michael S. Lasky, *The Complete Films of Alfred Hitchcock* (New York: Citadel Press, 1995), 223.

31. Freeland, "Natural Evil," 62.

32. Cohen, *Hitchcock's Cryptonymies, Volume II*, 151, 153.

33. Scott Calef, "Featherless Bipeds: The Concept of Humanity in *The Birds*," in *Hitchcock and Philosophy: Dial M for Metaphysics*, eds. David Baggett and William A. Drumin (Chicago: Open Court Publishing, 2007), 84.

34. Elisabeth Weis, *The Silent Scream: Alfred Hitchcock's Sound Track* (Rutherford, NJ: Fairleigh Dickinson University Press, 1982), 144.

35. Richard Allen, *Hitchcock's Romantic Irony* (New York: Columbia University Press, 2007), 233.

36. Robin Wood, *Hitchcock's Films Revisited* (New York: Columbia University Press, 1989), 166.

37. Kay Sloan, "Three Hitchcock Heroines: The Domestication of Violence," *New Orleans Review* 12, no. 4 (winter 1985): 94.

38. Richard Allen, "Avian Metaphor in *The Birds*," *Hitchcock Annual* 6 (1997-98), 51.

39. Dan Auiler, *Hitchcock's Notebooks: An Authorized and Illustrated Look Inside the Creative Mind of Alfred Hitchcock* (New York: Avon Books, 1999), 390.

40. François Truffaut, *Hitchcock* (New York: Simon and Schuster, 1984), 287.

41. Allen, *Hitchcock's Romantic Irony,* 228.

42. Truffaut, *Hitchcock,* 254.

43. Allen, "Hitchcock and the Wandering Woman," 150.

44. Auiler, *Hitchcock's Notebooks,* 391.

45. John Hellmann, "*The Birds* and the Kennedy Era," *Hitchcock Annual* 17 (2011): 104.

46. Hellmann, "*The Birds* and the Kennedy Era," 104-05.

47. Wood, *Hitchcock's Films Revisited,* 163.

48. Hunter, "Me and Hitch," Sight and Sound 7, no. 6 (June 1997): 31.

49. John P. McCombe, " 'Oh, I See . . .': *The Birds* and the Culmination of Hitchcock's Hyper-Romantic Vision," *Cinema Journal* 44, no. 3 (spring 2005): 75.

50. Christopher Sharrett, "The Myth of Apocalypse and the Horror Film: The Primacy of *Psycho* and *The Birds*," *Hitchcock Annual* 4 (1995-96): 50.

51. Hunter, "Me and Hitch," 32.

52. Raymond Durgnat, *The Strange Case of Alfred Hitchcock; or, The Plain Man's Hitchcock* (Cambridge: Massachusetts Institute of Technology Press, 1974), 336.

53. Ian Cameron and Richard Jeffrey, "The Universal Hitchcock," in *A Hitchcock Reader,* eds. Marshall Deutelbaum and Leland Poague (Ames: Iowa State University Press, 1986), 267.

54. Bernard F. Dick, "Hitchcock's Terrible Mothers," *Literature/Film Quarterly* 28, no. 4 (2000): 243.

55. Sharrett, "The Myth of Apocalypse," 51.

56. Neil P. Hurley, *Soul in Suspense: Hitchcock's Fright and Delight* (Metuchen, New Jersey: Scarecrow Press, 1993), 3.

57. Harris and Lasky, *Complete Films,* 223.

58. Durgnat, *Strange Case,* 338.

59. Tom Cohen, *Hitchcock's Cryptonymies, Volume I: Secret Agents* (Minneapolis: University of Minnesota Press, 2005), 224; emphasis in original. An additional failure of technology can be seen in the automobile that Melanie cannot use to drive away from the attack, because the keys are missing.

60. David Sterritt, *The Films of Alfred Hitchcock* (New York: Cambridge University Press, 1993), 142; emphasis in original.

61. Camille Paglia, *The Birds* (London: British Film Institute Press, 1998), 73.

62. Martyn Shawcross, *The Private World of Daphne du Maurier* (London: Robson Books, 1991), 144.

63. Walter Isaacson, *Einstein: His Life and Universe* (New York: Simon and Schuster, 2008), 494.

64. Slavoj Žižek, " 'In His Bold Gaze My Ruin Is Writ Large,' " in *Everything You Always Wanted to Know About Lacan (But Were Afraid to Ask Hitchcock),* ed. Slavoj Žižek (London: Verso, 1992), 256.

65. Susan Smith, *Hitchcock: Suspense, Humour, and Tone* (London: British Film Institute Publishing, 2000), 129.

66. Margaret Horwitz, "*The Birds*: A Mother's Love," *Wide Angle: A Film Quarterly of Theory, Criticism, and Practice* 5, no. 1 (1982): 46.

67. Raja Halwani and Steven Jones, "*The Birds*: Plato and Romantic Love," in *Hitchcock and Philosophy: Dial M for Metaphysics,* 70.

68. Conrad, *The Hitchcock Murders,* 39.

69. Michael Walker, *Hitchcock's Motifs* (Amsterdam: Amsterdam University Press, 2005), 128.

70. Peter Bogdanovich, *The Cinema of Alfred Hitchcock,* 44.

71. Wood, *Hitchcock's Films Revisited,* 172.

72. Dora Beale Polk, *The Island of California: A History of the Myth* (Spokane, Washington: Arthur H. Clark, 1991), 332.

73. Richard Schickel, "Hitchcock on Hitchcock: An Interview," in *Perspectives on Alfred Hitchcock,* ed. David Boyd (New York: G.K. Hall, 1995), 36.

74. Alfred Hitchcock, "On Style," in *Hitchcock on Hitchcock,* 294-95.

APARNA FRANK

Tamil Hitchcock:
Sundaram Balachander's The Doll (1964)

Many Indian filmmakers like Biren Nag, Mukul Anand, Raj Khosla, Vijay Anand, Vidhu Vinod Chopra, and Robby Grewal have remade and self-consciously evoked the cinema of Hitchcock to craft a vernacular mode of suspense.[1] To this list, one must add the subject of this essay, the South Indian Tamil filmmaker, actor, and composer, Sundaram Balachander (1927-90). Balachander deserves special attention in that he distinctly fashioned himself as a film auteur of suspense and mystery genres. Very little has been written about his films, but he is popularly known in Tamil cinema as "the Alfred Hitchcock of South India."[2] Like all sobriquets, the description is a bit of an exaggeration, and it truly testifies to how Hitchcock is deemed synonymous in the popular imagination with all kinds of detective and crime-oriented cinema. Nonetheless, the titular association with Hitchcock captures Balachander's fascination with suspense thrillers and whodunits, even if the latter were specifically rejected by Hitchcock. It may well be that the comparison with Hitchcock was self-proclaimed, given Balachander's predilection for superlative titles and self-aggrandizing statements.[3] Indeed, this trait also parallels Hitchcock's self-generated popularity with the public in the form of cameos and high visibility in the *Alfred Hitchcock Presents* television series.

As an autodidact, Balachander learned much about film from reading books on Hollywood filmmakers and seeing Western cinema.[4] Raised in a family that was deeply involved in film and Carnatic music, he made his first film appearance as a child actor in Vankudre Shantaram's production *Sita Kalyanam* (1933). His music and film career evolved simultaneously, and he took on several directing and acting roles in Tamil and Telugu films during the late forties and mid-fifties. Given that we know so little about Balachander's views on film, perhaps the most critical question that any biographer or film historian would have wanted to ask him was why he was drawn to suspense and mystery genres.

Without proposing causal explanations, I would like to offer some hypotheses on the background for Balachander's attraction to these genres. For instance, it is possible that he was exposed to Hitchcock's films and other British and American films on which he based his own cinema through his deep involvement with the local Cine Technician's Association, where foreign films were screened.[5] My second hypothesis draws upon Balachander's reputation as an accomplished chess player and his interest in constrained writing, an experimental form in which a self-imposed creative rule such as the omission of certain alphabets or the substitution of one alphabet for another invites the reader to engage with the text as a riddle or a code. Balachander's first chess-problem was composed at the age of ten and published in the national newspaper in 1937.[6] Chess, in the form of a composition or puzzle is analogous to detective/mystery fiction in that it involves "retrograde" reasoning.[7] That is, the solution for the problem/puzzle is arrived at by retracing and reimagining (within the norms provided by the author of the puzzle) the steps leading to the proposed problem. The authors and solvers of chess puzzles are thus fittingly described as aesthetes who appreciate the intrinsic beauty and complexity of the test itself and the economy with which it demands to be solved. In a similar fashion, Balachander's letters to his family are amusing exercises in constrained writing in the form of lipograms and calligrams.[8] The intricate and meticulous patterns displayed in these letters reveal a mind drawn to logical and analytical conundrums. Constrained writing and chess compositions can also be seen as the kind of rule-driven play that Thomas Leitch, drawing upon Roger Caillois' taxonomies, identifies generally as "ludic" in Hitchcock's cinema.[9] Visual puzzles, cameo appearances, and metaphors of games in Hitchcock's films invite the spectator to participate not simply in the resolution of the diegetic problem *per se* but in decoding an aesthetic challenge for its own merits and appreciating the technique or wit with which it is constructed.

Many of Balachander's films draw upon situations, motifs, and subgenres that are found in Hitchcock's *oeuvre*, namely, espionage, the Gothic, and the wrong-man thriller. His most famous work, *Andha Naal* (*That Day*, 1954), made for AVM studios, is an espionage-whodunit with echoes of *Sabotage* (1936), in that a wife is accused of murdering her unpatriotic husband. However, it is primarily inspired by Kurosawa's *Rashomon* (1950) and Anthony Asquith's *The Woman in Question* (1950). The film's novelty in the context of Indian cinema is that it lacked songs. The felicitous irony that a musician was the author of such an innovation has often served to endorse Balachander's reputation as a maverick in Tamil cinema. Under his short-lived production company, S.B. Creations (1962-70), Balachander directed and acted in three films for which he is most remembered: *Avana Ivan* (*Is He the One?* 1962), *Bommai* (*The Doll*, 1964), and *Nadu Iravil* (*In the Dead of Night*, 1970). These films have their sources in British and American films. Based on *A Place in the Sun* (1951), *Avana Ivan* lends itself to comparison with *Strangers on a Train* (1951). The film's anti-hero protagonist, played by Balachander, murders his fiancée to marry a wealthy woman. His last film, *Nadu Iravil*, was based on Agatha Christie's *And Then There Were None* (1939) and was perhaps one of the first Tamil films in the Gothic horror genre.

Balachander's experimental approach to music and his highly interactive engagement with the listener during performances shed some light on his style as a filmmaker.[10] For instance, he follows Hitchcock in using suspense to play with audience expectation, but he also intensifies that mode of address by breaking the fourth wall. In *Avana Ivan*, the title sequence, a stylized montage of the protagonist's face in close-up, is introduced almost forty-five minutes into the film, and after the murder of the fiancée. Similarly, in *Nadu Iravil*, the entire cast is introduced soon after the exposition of the film's diegetic conflict. These gimmicks and novelties nonetheless are not qualitatively comparable with Hitchcock's artistic and sophisticated practice of "pure cinema." While Hitchcockian aesthetics is a testament to his beginnings in silent film and his affirmation of the essence of the medium as visual storytelling and montage, Balachander was not even remotely interested in severing Tamil cinema's ties to theater. Ultimately his images were what Hitchcock derisively described as "photographs of people talking."

Given the very little research and commentary on Balachander's cinema apart from newspaper articles, a recent biography, and blog entries, in my essay I aim to offer an introductory analysis of the film that best illustrates his reputation as a "Hitchcockian" filmmaker. The adjective "Hitchcockian" has often been associated with his film *Bommai* and the film's relationship to Hitchcock's *Sabotage* (1936), an adaptation of Joseph Conrad's novel *The Secret Agent: A Simple Tale* (1907).[11] It is hard to ascertain if Balachander discussed Hitchcock's cinema and *Sabotage* in particular with his screenwriter, Vidwan V. Lakshmanan. While I have found evidence of a hand-painted Indian poster for *Sabotage*, only further research can confirm if the film was screened in Madras and before the making of *Bommai*.[12] However, upon viewing the two films it is clear that *Sabotage*'s bomb-sequence in which a boy, Stevie, is entrusted to deliver a package of film reels that unknown to him contains a bomb is the dominant motivation for *Bommai*. In *Sabotage* the audience knows there is a bomb that will shortly explode, but Stevie does not. Having made us fear for Stevie's life, Hitchcock contrived to blow him up, a decision for which he was roundly criticized.

Susan Smith defends Hitchcock against the viewing public's opprobrium by arguing for his "avoidance of cliché" as a key creative factor that explains his decision to confirm the spectator's worst fears.[13] But clichés can also be avoided when ensuring that the principals are protected because the spectator in a suspense sequence is not only engaged in the ultimate outcome of the events but also speculates on *how* (than simply *whether*) the filmmaker will creatively resolve the situation. The interest in the method of relieving suspense throws a different light on Hitchcock's regret at the Stevie sequence: he conned the audience in the game of suspense.

Balachander's objective in *Bommai* is to correct Hitchcock's "error" by prolonging the enjoyment of suspense and in that process protect the innocent victims and punish the wrong-doers. His correction of *Sabotage* is therefore not anti-Hitchcockian or even a morally motivated revision of the Stevie sequence, for he appears to take much pleasure in incorporating and introducing to Tamil cinema the more ludic, darkly humorous, and ambivalent aspects of Hitchcockian aesthetics such as suspense, chase, and the playful interaction of the filmmaker with the spectator. Thus, if Hitchcock "sabotaged" Conrad's text for his "cinematic ends," as Paula Marantz Cohen states, then Balachander's correction of Hitchcock's "sabotage" is also a creative and cinematically inspired outcome of his exploitation of Hitchcockian aesthetics.[14]

Bommai replaces *Sabotage*'s suggestive dissolves, the ambiguous representation of Verloc's murder, and Hitchcock's reflexive use of the cinema hall and the film reels with formulaic idioms of Indian cinema: song and dance numbers for popular appeal, slapstick humor, theatrical performances, and stereotypical villain and vamp. The film is also fairly conventional in lacking the complex characterization that is suggested in Balachander's other Hitchcockian works, *Avana Ivan* and *Andha Naal*, where the anti-hero protagonists are reminiscent of Uncle Charlie in *Shadow of a Doubt* (1943) or Bruno in *Strangers on a Train*.

The story of *Bommai* concerns the departure of a wealthy businessman, Somasundaram, to Singapore. His business partner, Jagadish, who remains in Madras, has hatched a plot with Prabhakar, a scientist, to murder Somasundaram during his stay in Singapore. Jagadish's motivations are twofold: he wants to usurp the business from Somasundaram and sabotage Somasundaram's mission in Singapore, which concerns verifying certain claims about Jagadish's shady past as an escaped murderer in Singapore. Having intercepted the letter that Somasundaram received about his criminal history with the help of his lover-secretary, Nalini, who plays the conventional vamp, Jagadish masterminds a bomb-plot with the help of Prabhakar. To execute his plot, Jagadish has formed an underworld gang made up of disgruntled employees who feel that they have been treated like slaves by Somasundaram. Prabhakar, the parallel to the Professor in *Sabotage,* conceals the bomb inside a doll.[15]

Jagadish's plan is to ask Somasundaram to deliver the doll as a gift to a friend in Singapore. The rationale is that Somasundaram will retrieve the address-note that has been stitched into the lining of the doll's dress and this will trigger the bomb to which it is connected, thus killing him. However, in an unexpected turn of events, Mani and Sampath, the comic members of the gang who are in charge of delivering the doll to Somasundaram in the airport, leave the doll behind in a cab. The misplaced doll/bomb passes through the hands of children, vagrants, cab drivers, and even the police. It is pursued by Jagadish and his gang, followed by the conscientious defectors from the gang, and in the end by the police as well. Following a series of missed and serendipitous encounters, the doll finds its way back to Jagadish and kills him and the members of his gang.

In its final scene, *Bommai* explicitly articulates its difference from the central situation in *Sabotage.* Expressing his concern over the danger the bomb has caused for the public, Somasundaram asks the policeman if the bomb has been defused. The policeman replies, "the bomb has exploded where it has to and it has killed the people it is supposed to." By pointing to the "appropriate" release of suspense (the "correct" targets of the bomb), the policeman's words directly reference the "errors" in the Stevie sequence and underline *Bommai*'s revision of that sequence in a reflexive fashion. In what follows, I analyze *Bommai*'s revision of the Stevie sequence by drawing attention to its selective emphasis on certain Hitchcockian strategies. In the first section, I discuss Hitchcockian suspense and the chase as enabling the redemption of Stevie in *Bommai* by means of prolonging the potential for what Hitchcock described as "the enjoyment of fear" over "terror."[16] The second section examines how the "invisible cloak of protection" that Hitchcock defined as an assumption or contract between the director and the audience ensuring the safety of the imperiled innocent principals is represented by Balachander's playful engagement with the spectator.[17]

The Rhetoric of Adventure: Chase and Suspense in Bommai

Unlike the political intrigue that serves as the solemn backdrop for Verloc's motivations and actions in *Sabotage*, *Bommai* constructs a personal narrative that unfolds in the form of a chase with several levels of interlocking action. Illustrating Hitchcock's definition of the chase as fundamental to cinema, the two lines of action in *Bommai*, infused with a light comedic touch, concern the pursuit of the bomb and the circulation of the bomb among various members of the public.[18] And just as multiple chases are featured in numerous films by Hitchcock, the hunt for the bomb in *Bommai* is undertaken by three sets of characters whose actions eventually overlap. The first set includes Mani and Sampath, the characters responsible for losing the doll/bomb, who seek to retrieve it before it reaches the hands of Anandan, a co-worker who defects from the gang once he learns of Jagadish's plot. Later, Mani and Sampath also set out to entrap Anandan and prevent him from contacting the police. The second set includes the lovers, Anandan and Mallika (Prabhakar's sister), who represent the morally upright group that is concerned with the public's safety. They are also attempting to inform the police of the assassination plot. The third set of characters who track the doll is a motley bunch of the public and the police – a street urchin, the cab driver Manickam, in whose cab the doll was left behind, and Mallika. Once Mallika and

Anandan chance upon Manickam the cab driver the various search parties swiftly track the whereabouts of the doll/bomb and the chase sequences get shorter, as Hitchcock prescribed, as the narrative moves towards the climax.

All these multiple pursuits parallel the kind of deferral-of-the climax chase that Leitch describes as an excuse for entertainment in *To Catch a Thief* (1955), and on a more serious level, they resemble the futile actions of the searchers (Scotland Yard) and the hunted (Verloc) in *Sabotage*.[19] For instance, in one scene, both Mani and Sampath fail to retrieve the doll that is returned to the cab driver by arguing that not all dolls are dolls with bombs. Similarly, Mallika and Anandan fail to investigate the doll in the hands of a poor vagrant by stating that it is unlikely for an expensive doll to be found in his possession. One would suppose that it is precisely the oddity of a blind vagrant caught with an expensive doll that would raise suspicions. Moreover, the gang that should know better falls victim to its own scheme when it repurchases the doll from a toyshop believing that it is a new one. All of the search parties are inept at retrieving the first doll/bomb. This leads the gang to hatch a second bomb-plot with a new doll. Equally, the scenes showing the comic duo's search for the bomb amongst cab drivers serve primarily as comic relief. Many farcical jokes and verbal puns are exchanged to leaven the tense sequences with the bomb. The searchers awkwardly ask cab drivers if explosions have occurred in the city and the cab drivers respond with descriptions of explosions caused by car tires and colliding vehicles. The bathetic response is also intended to disappoint the spectator whose curiosity is momentarily aroused when the cab drivers claim that an explosion had indeed occurred. Ultimately, the doll eludes the searchers by reaching a toy store, and Somasundaram is saved only because he accidentally leaves his bag in Manickam's cab, which leads Manickam to get to the airport and inform him of Jagadish's plans. Finally, the police, typically portrayed as inept in Indian cinema, as is the case in Hitchcock's films, arrive late and are unable to prevent the first bomb from exploding and killing the gang. Thus the chase's underlying function is to thwart the deterministic overtones that are implicit in the linear, race-against-time structure of the Stevie sequence. Structurally, the chase sequences serve as a useful buffer for the shots that heighten the sense of an impending explosion.

Notwithstanding the superficiality of the pursuit, several sequences in the film do exemplify Hitchcock's prescriptions for a good cinematic chase. First, the misplacement of the bomb in the cab functions as the springboard situation that Hitchcock described as the event that sets off the suspense from the first-reel, "letting the audience into the secret as early as possible."[20] Here the departure from *Sabotage* is crucial. Unlike Stevie, who is delayed and distracted by the events of the Lord Mayor's show, in *Bommai,* it is the bomb that deviates from its target and is made to wander in the city. The springboard situation thus diverts the attention from the agent to the object. The springboard situation in *Bommai* is also analogous to the structure of Hitchcock's television show, *Bang! You're Dead,* where the young boy Jackie leaves home with a loaded gun that threatens an unknowing public.[21] Second, true to Hitchcock's recurrent emphasis on the close affinity between motion picture and moving vehicles, Balachander implicates the car and even the plane as "machines" that facilitate chaos (as seen in the breakdown of the car and the explosion of the gang in the car) and the restoration of order (Manickam the cab driver informs Somasundaram of the bomb plot in the end).[22] The location shots of the careening police jeep and the gang's car must have appealed to audiences of that time as an exciting effect of the motion picture's innate affinity to moving vehicles. Third, the alternation between the searchers and the circuit of the doll/bomb among children illustrates in a highly entertaining and clever manner Hitchcock's observation that the multiple-chase format allows the spectator to "run with the hare and hunt with the hounds." We "enjoy the fear" that is generated by the elusive doll/bomb while following the twists and turns in the chase that lead to the resolution.

In the opening section of the film, the chase is a race for getting the doll to Somasundaram at the airport in time. The very first shot of the film—a close-up of a clock showing the time as 9 A.M.—reminds us of the Stevie sequence in *Sabotage*. When Mallika almost learns of her brother's plot, we see the clock hands at 9:35 behind them. The clock's prominence in the sequence makes us root for Jagadish's plan to succeed purely in terms of a race-against-time. As the sequence progresses, our excitement increases when we anticipate hurdles from Mallika, who has grown suspicious of her brother, and Mani and Sampath, whose   comic comportment   belies their competence in carrying out the bomb-plot. When the gang's car breaks down, the strategic disruption further amplifies our interest in the timely delivery of the fatal device. Then, as if to chastise us for our participation in this deadly scheme, Balachander has Mani and Sampath accidentally leave the doll behind in the cab. While this race to deliver the bomb is radically different from the Stevie sequence in its emphasis on the race as an event in the service of creating a thrilling effect, as opposed to deepening our identification with a character, it has already introduced Hitchcockian ambivalence in inviting the spectator to participate in a morally tainted yet exciting and suspenseful adventure.

Quite interestingly, *Bommai* contains many shots of the clock to mark the progression of the time, and the film also concludes with an image of the clock showing 5 P.M. This invocation of time seems to underline the overall design of the film's actions as having unfolded in one day between 9 a.m. and 5 P.M. The accent on the hours, arguably a novelty in Indian cinema at that time, reflects the kind of formal restriction that Balachander has set for himself – to make a film in which the action occurs within a day. Hitchcock too was intrigued by the challenges of constrained temporal filmmaking, as we see in such films as *Rope* (1948) and *The Trouble with Harry* (1955), and he also mentioned on numerous occasions his desire to make an entire film revolving around one day in the life of a city.[23]

Central to *Bommai*'s unsuccessful chase and the prolongation of suspense is the modification to the temporal component in *Sabotage*'s bomb. The fact that the explosion is set to occur at 1:45 P.M. in *Sabotage* means that suspense is predicated upon a race (temporal finish line) that in turn accentuates the sense of inevitability concerning Stevie's fate. By contrast, the bomb in *Bommai* is first explained as triggered by the act of pulling the address card from the doll. However, once the bomb is misplaced, Prabhakar confesses that the bomb could be set off in other ways, such as the very act of winding the doll or any kind of mishandling of it. In replacing the particular parameter of a time bomb with a vague condition, the scope for situational suspense and delayed release is broadened and the possibility of a non-explosion is exploited. Balachander's strategic alteration of the device along with the misplacement of the bomb is very much like a retrograde analysis in chess problems. That is, he attempts to redress *Sabotage*'s bomb sequence by retracing and changing the conditions of the source of the problem, which happens to be the temporal restriction in the time-bomb.

Besides the obvious reason that any sequence involving a bomb is suspense-worthy and thrill-friendly, Balachander's fascination with *Sabotage*'s bomb-sequence seems to hang on its iconographic distinction: the juxtaposition of a fatal weapon with an archetypal symbol of innocence. A variety of scenes in *Sabotage* similarly shows children in close proximity to a bomb. As Stevie carries the film reels to Piccadilly Circus, we see other children in the crowd stand beside him and close to the film reels. Similarly, when Mrs. Verloc walks into the movie theater after Stevie's death she is shown amidst the company of laughing children who are watching the violent cartoon "Who Killed Cock Robin?" Earlier in the film, when Mr. Verloc visits the bomb-maker/bird-shop owner, his interaction with the bomb-maker is intercut with shots of the bomb-maker's granddaughter. The bomb-maker's granddaughter, like Stevie, is also imperiled, in that her toys are interspersed with the ingredients for her grandfather's explosives. However, not all of these scenes function strictly as thematic and dramatic motivations but rather as as an impetus for Balachander to choose a doll as the vehicle for the bomb: encasing a bomb in a doll makes it a magnet for threatening situations involving children. Children in *Bommai* are not finely individualized like their predecessor, Stevie. Their presence heightens suspense and adds a touch of deviant humor, based on a startling alliance of children and bombs. Balachander recognizes that children as a special type of victim automatically provoke extreme shock and sympathy. Analogous to Eisenstein's arousal of fear through the infant in the baby carriage in the Odessa Steps sequence in *Battleship Potemkin*, he shows that as symbols of innocence children lend themselves for effortless emotional manipulation in the spectator. Thus the relative absence of individualization for Stevie's surrogates confirms that Balachander's suspense is crafted in adherence to the formulaic definition of Hitchcockian suspense, the asymmetry in knowledge between spectator and character over a ticking time-bomb.[24] In this sense, it could be argued that the entire film is an homage to Hitchcock's definition of suspense, and in particular, the example he used to illustrate it. Like the race to deliver the bomb, suspense is exploited in a purely formal manner in *Bommai*, as Hitchcock himself did in *Bang! You're Dead*.

The game of suspense is launched through what Leitch notes as a "contractual boundary" that guarantees the ensuing thrills.[25] Both Hitchcock and Balachander rely on objects to establish the contract. For instance, in *Bang! You're Dead*, extreme close-ups of Jackie loading the bullets and pointing the gun at the camera can be taken as visual acknowledgments of the spectator as a participant in the game of suspense. In a similar fashion, when Prabhakar explains to the gang how the bomb operates, the almost clinical exposition of the bomb's placement within the doll implies that the spectator is the intended addressee of the information (fig. 1). The shot alerts the audience to the rules of the game, for the information conveyed in this shot will be crucially and repeatedly recalled for the suspenseful

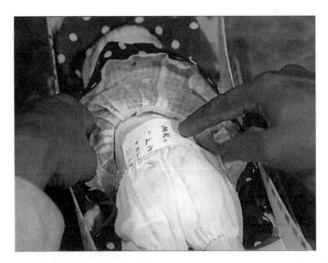

Figure 1

sequences. Balachander also uses the contract for humorous ends. In one scene, the pursuers believe that a cab driver is in possession of the doll. Balachander shows them opening the box containing the doll in extreme close-up and deliberately in a slow pace. The box turns out to contain a shoe, but the red herring confirms the self-conscious use of suspense as a game and the spectator as the recipient of the joke.

The first suspense sequence involves a couple who steal the doll from Manickam's cab for their daughter. The couple argues over the theft of the doll. In typical Hitchcockian fashion, Balachander uses their argument to frame the spectator's opposing interests. On the one hand, given our knowledge of the bomb, we side with the pleading husband whose powerlessness against his wife mirrors our helplessness as morally upright spectators who can only hope for the prevention of an onscreen catastrophe. But on the other hand, as thrill-seekers we surreptitiously approve the theft, for it whets the appetite for suspense. Our tension is both prolonged and intensified when Balachander cuts to a different sequence and strategically introduces the shot of Prabhakar informing Jagadish and the others that the doll

Figure 2

could explode with any kind of mishandling. In the next shot, with the added knowledge of the bomb's unpredictable make-up, we see the father wind the doll aggressively in a manner that contradicts the warning mentioned by Prabhakar. The couple leaves the child alone with the doll as she winds it and briefly looks into the camera, confirming the perverse alliance that has been meticulously arranged for our view (fig. 2). The doll emits a whirring sound that implies the bomb has been triggered, all the while the girl keeps the doll close to her ears. When she asks her father about the sound, he dismisses her question by stating that the walking-doll might possess other "special characteristics," and encourages her to play with it without fear. This innuendo is intended for the spectator. The whirring stops and the girl continues to shake the doll, much to the alarm of the viewer. She then plays with the doll by singing a song in which she addresses the doll as her young sister.

The entire song sequence is composed of high- and low-angle, close-up, and extreme close-up shots of the doll as it walks, falls, and is placed in close proximity to the face of the child. Intercut with these scenes are shots of the couple who delight in their daughter's song. At the end of the song, the doll falls, and the whirring sound recurs. The camera tracks in to her face against the doll and primes the spectator for a rather macabre and visceral representation of horror. The sequence ends rather abruptly with the narrative shifting to the actions of the searchers. Balachander's use of close-up in this sequence is comparable to the superimposition of the "Don't Forget the Birds will sing at 1:45" in *Sabotage*. It arouses fear by means of a direct reminder, and shows, as Susan Smith notes, that "the real target of the attack," is the spectator.[26] Accordingly, the sequence, like *Sabotage*, instills in the spectator an awareness of the artifice that structures fear and anxiety. The dualism between involvement and detachment, as Smith perceptively notes, endows the spectator with a parental perspective on the imperiled characters, who in the case of both *Sabotage* and *Bommai* are literally children. While we are afraid for the girl, just as we are for Stevie in *Sabotage*, we are also aware of the "mechanisms and processes" (the song, and the close-ups of the doll) that mediate our "self-consciousness about being positioned outside of the narrative world."[27] This ambivalent point of view is further complicated by the dark humor that is blatantly provoked through the disconcerting use of the song in *Bommai*.

The music in the Stevie sequence in *Sabotage* captures a range of tones that begin with light humor and optimism (the upbeat band music of the parade) but eventually convey fear. Once Stevie enters the bus, the sense of entrapment and the escalation of time are fully supported by a tense and foreboding score that in many ways prepares the spectator for the catastrophe. By contrast, the song that is diegetically placed (sung by a character) in *Bommai* prolongs the suspense for almost three and a half minutes. In any other sequence, the song might be seen as a clichéd "harmless" convention, but in deploying that very conventionality for an unconventional situation, Balachander exploits the spectator's knowledge of the song's incommensurability with the situation for a perverse effect. This gesture discloses Balachander's taste for Hitchcockian dark humor that we see in the laughter that follows Stevie's demise (after the explosion there is a quick and disturbing cut to Mr. Verloc, Mrs. Verloc, and Ted all laughing, oblivious to what just happened) and the odd but ultimately revealing use of a cartoon (*Who Killed Cock Robin?*) as both a mirror of sorrow and as an omen of Verloc's death. Similar to the cartoon's rhetorical function, the song in *Bommai* has no diegetic purpose except for prolonging suspense and flaunting its unsettling inappropriateness for the situation. Moreover, the ambiguity in *Bommai*'s song sequence resides in visually presenting a threatening situation through the close-ups of the doll and in aurally offering a cheerful melody. If we enjoy the song by forgetting the bomb, we are irresponsible parental surrogates, but if we are too concerned with fear and ignore the song, we miss the humor.

The second suspense sequence is associated with a different pattern of Hitchockian suspense. We are introduced to a five-year-old boy celebrating his birthday with his friends. The *mise-en-scène* indicates that the boy belongs to a wealthy family. The boy's mother indulges him with a celebratory song. Before the beginning of this song and during its course, Balachander introduces a detail that complicates our interest in the birthday scene. He shows an urchin boy looking into the birthday party from outside the mansion. The urchin asks the birthday boy to share his ice cream but he is brushed away, and the song that ensues is intercut with a shot of him hungrily peeping into the party.

Except for vague portents of another suspenseful situation involving children and the bomb, the purpose behind this sequence is withheld from the spectator and revealed only at the end of it. The delayed exposition draws on a variation of Hitchcockian suspense that relies on the concealment of information from the spectator. Smith interprets this pattern by citing sequences from *Frenzy* and *Spellbound* that briefly mislead the spectator into thinking that Blaney is the necktie killer and that Ballantine has killed Dr. Brulov.[28] But the sequence that is closer to the kind of inference that we are invited to make in *Bommai* is the crop-duster scene in *North by Northwest*. Our knowledge of Eve Kendall's complicity with

Figure 3

Vandamm gives us a presentiment of what awaits Thornhill, but we are generally unaware of the form the threat will assume. Consequently, we are also less emotionally involved. Balachander exercises a similar form of suppressive suspense by rousing our curiosity (rather than fear) about how the sequence will tie in with the circulating doll. It is only when the camera pulls back at the end of the song sequence to show Manickam greeting the birthday boy and his mother with the doll that the conventional suspense come into effect. We are now anxious for the children in the party and the urchin who has shifted his attention from the feast to the doll.

This sequence ups the ante because it is a room full of children who are now endangered (fig. 3). The setting suggests a possible inspiration from or a parallel to Cathy Brenner's birthday party scene in *The Birds* (1964). As noted in the sequence with the girl and the doll, soon after Manickam gives the doll to the boy, Balachander cuts to a different sequence in the plot as a way of heightening the tension. When he returns to the scene of the birthday party, the possibility of a massacre is suggested in the sound and image of children gathered around the doll. The wound-up doll walks and stumbles, and as in the earlier instance, the whirring sound is heard. But this time, instead cutting away, Balachander shows us the urchin boy who had been eyeing the doll now grab it and exit the frame. Our worries are now fully transferred to him. The third sequence of suspense shows the urchin boy and his friends in a slum. As he winds the doll, a policeman threatens to arrest them for their vagrancy. The children hide behind a bush as the doll falls and triggers the sound again. The spectator believes that the doll is about to explode, but a dog runs in and whisks it away. In comparison to the first two sequences, the duration of suspense for this sequence is considerably reduced.

The film's final illustration of suspense occurs at a setting that is also evocative of Hitchcockian irony. This time the doll is wound up by a police officer who finds it among a heap of stolen goods. He shakes the doll, stating that it is unusually heavy, and makes the doll walk on his desk. For one last time we are invited to experience the deeply ironic possibility of a bomb explosion caused by an agent of law: a figure that is meant to protect the characters from danger. As is typical by now, the doll does not explode and it is wrongfully claimed by a toy shop owner.

The spectator's response to the last two instances of suspense is quite different from the first two. While in the previous examples a genuine fear of an explosion was aroused, in the last two sequences the spectator is less afraid and more convinced that the bomb will not explode. The source for the spectator's flagging conviction in the doll as a credible source of threat can be attributed to two distinct features. The first is that, contrary to all signs of an impending explosion (the whirring sound and the abuse of the doll), the bomb is inexplicably not triggered. The actions of the agents who (mis)handle the doll fail to cause the effect that is forewarned by Prabhakar. Perhaps this is a malfunctioning of the device. However, given that the "malfunction" occurs at the end of every suspense sequence, it acquires a protective characteristic and contributes to the spectator's loss of fear and, indeed, perverse disappointment over the absence of an onscreen explosion.

Second, the policeman and the dog, as thinly disguised figures of rescue, assure us that the bomb is an elusive object. The policeman and the dog are instrumental for keeping the doll/bomb in circulation, which automatically entails not harming the children. The relatively short shot duration for the last two suspense sequences thus privileges chase and adventure over fear. Once we understand these signs as elements of artifice, suspense becomes quite literally a *vieux jeu* to which the spectator has grown accustomed.

The change in the status of the doll/bomb resembles the irreverential treatment of Harry's corpse (the corpse that never goes away) as shown in its serial disinterments in *The Trouble with Harry*. Like Harry's corpse, the bomb also becomes less fearful once its elusiveness becomes apparent. Furthermore, paralleling the staged repositioning of Harry's corpse in the same location for Sheriff Wiggs's discovery, the doll/bomb returns to the gang where it is "rediscovered" as the original doll. The circular design of both films enables the diffusion of the threat to the community (prior to its literal containment) by means of repetition and the frustration of expectations. While we retain a curiosity in both films for how the problem that intrudes upon the community will be solved, we are assured that Harry's death and the bomb will not implicate and threaten that community. That curiosity is "satisfied" with the bathetic framing of Harry's death as an uneventful or natural affair, and in *Bommai* the bomb's release is reserved for the conventional karmic ending of good winning over evil.

The Rhetoric of Reassurance: Games in Bommai

While the futile chase and the replication of safe suspense implicitly hint at the insulation of the innocent principals, it is Balachander's embrace of game-playing as a director and his representation of the doll as a plaything that complete the film's redemptive modification of *Sabotage*'s bomb sequence. He takes the cue for the game from the one played between the characters in the film itself. Like *Sabotage, Bommai* does not contain literal games or the kind of encoded visual puzzles that John Roberts discovers in *The Wrong Man*, but both films can be seen as thematically and formally structured around the game of hide-and-seek and its central ingredient: deception.[29] For example, the chase in *Bommai* is predicated upon the doll being hidden from its pursuers and in the pursuers being poor players of hide-and-seek. They fail to search the doll even when it is in their hands.

Deception also describes the way objects (film reels, the doll), locations (the Bijou Movie Theater, Spencer's grocery stand, the bird shop, Somasundaram's International Business House) and characters in both films espouse different identities to sustain the game of hide-and-seek. For that purpose, Balachander adopts Hitchcock's misleading representation of villains as excessively polite, genial figures (e.g., Verloc, Bruno in *Strangers on a Train* [1951], and Rusk in *Frenzy* [1972]) and protagonists as moody and irritable (e.g., Devlin in *Notorious* [1946], Jefferies in *Rear Window* [1954], and Blaney in *Frenzy*). Somasundaram is an unlikable figure even if he is the "victim" with whom we are supposed to sympathize. He instills fear in his employees and is controlling. He asks Sampath to quit the habit of playing harmonica, and his imperious comportment is symbolized in the way he uses his walking stick to interact with his employees like a strict schoolteacher. Jagadish, while essentially a stereotype, also has shades of the deceptive Hitchcockian villain. His genial temperament and smug confidence in the ingenuity of his scheme belie his sinister intentions and allow him to easily manipulate Somasundaram.

The treacherousness of the doll against the villains is hinted early on in the film when Prabhakar, in a somewhat Frankensteinian tone, asks the "doll" that he describes as his baby, "You won't betray me would you?" Similarly, in *Sabotage*, the extradiegetic associations of the title of the film that Stevie carries, *Batholomew the Strangler,* poignantly allude to the fate that befalls him. In contrast to both Ted Spencer and the bus driver's association of Stevie with the titular "strangler," "Bartholomew" as a historical figure connotes violence: the macabre martyrdom of Saint Bartholomew and the St. Bartholomew's Day Massacre. These associations hint at the figurative betrayal of Stevie as the sacrificed figure. Deception as instrumental for betrayal is established at the beginning of *Bommai* when Somasundaram mysteriously tells Jagadish that he remembers the incident that brought them together: during Japanese air raids in Burma, Jagadish saved Somasundaram's life by taking a bullet for his friend. The recollection of this incident reveals Somasundaram's guilt in undertaking a mission against a friend to whom he owes his life. Countering Somasundaram's betrayal is Jagadish, who is one step ahead of the game in having acquired information of the real purpose behind Somasundaram's mission. These diegetic instances of deception are in the end upstaged by the more calculated and pervasive act of hide-and-seek that Balachander plays, somewhat in the amusing vein of Hitchcock's cameos, as Somasundaram and director.

At first glance, we are tempted to find surrogates for Balachander within the film. Similar to Susan Smith's view that Verloc and the Professor are convincing surrogates of Hitchcock, the saboteur-artist, we can propose Jagadish and Prabhakar as Balachander's stand-ins.[30] Then there is Somasundaram, who displays his authority like a director yet is the victim of the bomb-plot. Why did Balachander cast himself as Somasundaram and not as Jagadish or Prabhakar? After all, given his fondness for antiheroes, he could have easily chosen the role of Jagadish or Prabhakar. I believe that in choosing Somasundaram as his role, Balachander's intentions were to mislead the spectator into thinking that he is the protagonist of the film. Given Balachander's reputation as a leading-man in earlier films, Tamil cinema audiences would have believed that Somasundaram is the central character. That expectation is overturned when Somasundaram disappears for a good portion of the film and his place is occupied by the children whose fate is controlled by Balachander the director. In contrast to Hitchcock's cameos, Balachander's self-effacing gesture is a joke played against his own screen presence. At the same

Figure 4

time, Balachander fully discloses the centrality of his directorial authority in a manner that is similar to Hitchcock's signature introductions and epilogues in *Alfred Hitchcock Presents*.

Following the last diegetic shot in the film, Balachander speaks to the audience as the director and proceeds to introduce on-camera the entire cast and crew in a theatrical manner (fig. 4). In the very last shot, he introduces the doll as the central character in the film. The bizarre end-credit sequence reminds the audience that the director is the author of the work and the direct address confirms that the principal participants of the game centered on the doll were the filmmaker and the spectator.

Like the children in *Bommai*, Balachander too, by casting himself as a courier for and victim of a bomb-plot assumes the nominal position of being Stevie's surrogate. Consequently, by separating at the outset Stevie's surrogate from the rest of the narrative, Balachander renders the bomb-plot and indeed his own presence as leading-man like a MacGuffin or a pretext for stimulating the chase and adventure. The bomb-plot to kill Somasundaram in *Bommai* is not a "pure MacGuffin" like the inconsequential microfilms in *North by Northwest*, for it is also critical for the resolution of the narrative. However, it is a barely concealed premise for the thrills that comprise the middle-portion of the film. Furthermore, unlike the Stevie sequence, the Somasundaram bomb-plot is a preoccupation for the principal characters but not for the audience, who have not been encouraged to identify with or develop sympathies for Somasundaram.

The strategic reappearance of Somasundaram close to the end of the film is another indicator of the bomb-plot as a "gimmick" (which is how Hitchcock described the MacGuffin).[31] While we believe that Somasundaram has boarded the plane to Singapore and escaped Jagadish's bomb-plot, he makes a surprising reentry, stating that his flight was cancelled due to mechanical failure. Interpreting the plane's breakdown as fate intervening against his clandestine mission, he confesses to Jagadish the purpose of his visit to Singapore and expresses remorse for suspecting his friend. He thus tells Jagadish that he is not prepared to return to Singapore to verify his innocence. However, once Jagadish learns that Somasundaram's flight is rescheduled for take-off in an hour, he uses it as an opportunity to launch a second bomb-plot and coaxes Somasundaram to visit Singapore as planned and confirm his innocence once and for all. Jagadish then asks Prabhakar to place another bomb in a new doll, which he hands over to Somasundaram to be delivered in Singapore.

Somasundaram's confession to Jagadish can be seen as a form of directorial exculpation from the act of betrayal and deception, but it also remarkably coincides with the spectator's loss in the credibility of the doll/bomb as a fear-inducing device in the last suspense sequences. It is as though our recognition of the doll/bomb too as a mere gimmick in the third and fourth suspense sequences is rather cleverly anticipated by Balachander and counterbalanced by the reintroduction of the original target. Somasundaram's reentry precipitates the closure of the narrative, but its true ingenuity lies in exposing the first bomb-plot and the doll as a purely formal device for adventure and suspense. His reappearance makes it abundantly clear that Balachander as Somasundaram hides or dons the "invisible cloak of protection" so that Balachander the director could play (and protect).

Like the duplicitous characters and objects, Balachander also has two opposing faces as the visible victim and the invisible protector. He ambitiously occupies both the sympathetic, powerless position of Stevie and the manipulative position of his playful rescuer. As a result of such a dualism, the predication of suspense and adventure upon the disappearance of Stevie's surrogate generates an interesting contradiction. That is, from the spectator's point of view, the price that Somasundaram pays for escaping the bomb-plot is the imperilment of children and the larger public. However, what appears as a leap from the fire into the frying pan for the spectator is in essence a widening of the playing field for the filmmaker in the form of the *deus ex machina*, or the invisible hand that controls the fate of characters and the continuation of the game.

Allen situates the upbeat and tragic outcomes of the *deus ex machina* (the "agency of Hitchcock," the narrator), in the conclusion of films such as *North by Northwest* and *Vertigo*.[32] In *Bommai*, the *deus ex machina* is operative throughout the film in the way it structures suspense and rescues the innocent principals. As mentioned before, the invisible hand cuts to another sequence whenever the bomb gives signs of exploding to evade the logical outcome that we expect. Also, by claiming through Prabhakar that the bomb *could* go off any minute, Balachander trades on that margin of possibility by not providing any reason at all for the non-explosion of the bomb despite the stated signs. Lastly, if Prabhakar and Jagadish rely on the comic minions for carrying out the bomb-plot, then the director uses those same minions to turn the bomb against them by showing them as childish adults who lack impulse control. In enacting what might be termed an elaborate narcissistic fantasy of both imperiling and rescuing himself and the surrogates of Stevie in the guise of the director, Balachander seems to suggest that only the *deus ex machina* could have saved Stevie in *Sabotage*.

While the outcome of Balachander's hidden agency is generally protective, it possesses a puckish quality (that Hitchcock would no doubt have appreciated) in conjoining the prolongation of suspense with the act of relieving suspense. For example, as we have seen, the *deus ex machina*, embedded in the misplacement of the bomb in the cab (literally a machine) saves Somasundaram only by occasioning more fear and excitement. Similarly, the suspense in the birthday party scene is relieved at the cost of endangering the urchin, and the game continues with the protection of the urchin and the policeman through the imperilment of the dog and the vagrant. Danger and safety are not mutually exclusive, and their intersection reflects the suspense-spectator's own position of desiring contradictory outcomes: the thrill of seeing the bomb triggered or an explosion onscreen and the need to protect innocent principals from such a catastrophe. And when the suspense is literally cut by the editorial hand, the viewer is disappointed. This sense of disappointment is critically exposed through one of the most sadistic uses of the *deus ex machina*.

After lulling the audience with a song sung by the blind vagrant, Balachander shocks us by showing the vagrant die in a car accident as he crosses the road with his dog and the doll. This baffling instance of auteurial intervention, again involving a machine, is a punitive move against the spectator who has anticipated an explosion during the film's other suspenseful sequences. The spectator is thus shamed into recognizing and disavowing that perverse desire by means of a gratuitous gesture. In the context of *Sabotage*, the vagrant's death illustrates what Hitchcock described as the appropriate strategy for the Stevie sequence—the surprising death of Stevie as opposed to a suspenseful one. Although the death of the vagrant is irreconcilably out of place given the film's overall avoidance of violence, it expresses, as in the Stevie sequence, the use of auteurial gamesmanship to slyly disclose to the spectator the lethal implications of the game played.

The sense of shock we experience for the vagrant's death is to a great extent predicated upon Balachander making the spectator forget that the doll is a bomb when it is in the hands of the vagrant. Hitchcock, unlike Balachander, does not represent the film-reels outside the framework of suspense and violence. Balachander's attempt at showing the bomb-device in a different light reveals a more playful treatment of the theme of deception and the player himself. For example, while the doll and the film reels are objects of terror and violence, in *Sabotage*, the bomb, by virtue of being concealed in a film reel, ends up tainting the auteur as a saboteur and even Stevie as well, given his love for the luridly titled film. One could of course interpret the film reels as mitigating the shock of Stevie's demise in reminding the audience that it is after all a game of suspense couched inside an illusion (the film). However, as Leitch argues, that game is played against the spectator by allowing the bomb to explode after the clock strikes 1:46 P.M.[33] Along the same lines, the explosion betrays the sense of pleasure and enjoyment associated with game-playing by giving the game of suspense a serious ending. Conversely, in *Bommai*, Balachander fully exploits the outward appearance of the bomb as a plaything to reassure the spectator that fear and danger are not the sole attributes of the doll.

Hitchcock adopted a similar strategy in *The Trouble with Harry* by demonstrating the lighter side of a possible murder through humor, wit, and a pleasant *mise-en-scène* that contrasts its macabre theme. Like the dualism of the doll/bomb, Harry's corpse too is framed both by Hitchcock and the characters as a less morbid object. Sam Marlowe's first perception of the corpse is as a model for his painting, and for Dr.Greenbow it is a negligible hindrance in his path. Similarly, Balachander projects the doll as a metaphor for his pet social and philosophical themes. In one scene, Manickam, the cab driver, exchanges the doll (which is shown as an expensive foreign-made toy) with his former employer for a doctor's recommendation to treat his ailing mother. It is made clear that the doll, like Harry's corpse, has a salubrious effect on the community. Even the close-ups of the doll in *Bommai*, while not overtly comical like the low-level close-ups of Harry's corpse, have the opposite effect of fear: they reinforce the bomb's innocuous identity as a doll. For example, the close-ups of the doll in the first suspense sequence can be taken in retrospect as a teasing invitation by Balachander to juggle the twin perceptions of the doll as an explosive and a toy. This dual perception is quite cleverly captured in the wordplay of the film's title: the first syllable in the Tamil word for "doll," "Bom," sounds like "bomb," a pun that audience members coming from an English-educated background in particular would recognize.

Throughout the film, the doll is also used to convey the tension between various classes in society. We see a hint of this sociological subtext in *Sabotage* when Mrs. Verloc finds the restaurant (Simpson's-in-the-Strand) that Spencer has taken her and Stevie to as above her means. Avrom Fleishman also notes that in providing a lower-middle-class décor for the Verlocs's domicile, Hitchcock, unlike Conrad, expresses a keen understanding of the hidden pressures of social class on the Verloc family.[34] In *Bommai*, class relationships are made evident through the doll's association with children from three different class structures.

The first girl's family represents a lower-middle class background. The second child comes from an upper-middle class family, and the third child is the urchin. As Susan Smith argues, when local forms of suspense detract our attention from the broader suspense narrative they offer "crucial insights into a film's deeper levels of significance."[35] In *Bommai*'s case, that distraction is manifested in the displacement of suspense to the urchin's role in the birthday scene. By intercutting the birthday scene shots of the hungry urchin (who is literally positioned outside the wealthy mansion) with his repeated looks at the party and the doll, Balachander indicates that his sympathies are strongly

Figure 5 (detail)

aligned with the disempowered (fig. 5). Interestingly, the urchin plays a critical role in informing the police of the pursuers.

A similar instance of meaningful distraction transpires in the sequence with the professor and his granddaughter in *Sabotage*. While the sequence in *Sabotage* has often been noted as a thematic companion to the Stevie sequence (both involving imperiled innocents), I find Hitchcock's portrayal of the Professor's daughter and granddaughter to be a haunting expression of defiance to the saboteurs (the Professor and Verloc). As in *Bommai,* Hitchcock's dual portrait of Verloc and the Professor is intercut with images of the woman and child. In the four shots devoted to them, we notice that they are distinguished from the garrulous Professor through their silence and their penetrating gaze at the Professor. They are unemotional but their looks almost seem accusatory in intent (fig. 6). Perhaps Hitchcock is suggesting that the Professor is responsible for the "cross" that his daughter "has to bear." Or he wants us to recall this image of the woman and her child at the end of the film, for they too, like Mrs.Verloc, are left destitute by a murderous saboteur. Like the surprising focus

Figure 6

on the urchin in *Bommai*, the combined silence of the woman and child and their uncanny stares shift our attention, however briefly, from the schemes of the saboteurs to the dismal lives of their unwitting accomplices and victims.

Balachander's humanism is overtly illustrated in the sequence with the vagrant, which also happens to be the film's most extended departure from suspense. Here, his unalloyed, representation of the doll as a plaything nudges the spectator to reflect on its symbolic attributes over its indiscernible content (the bomb). The irony that this demand for a shift in perception is brought through the figure of a blind vagrant is not lost on the spectator. Considered to be one of the most-talked about sequences in the film, the vagrant singer sits by a temple with the doll in his lap and sings a plaintive song with his Bulbul Tarang, a simple string instrument like a banjo[36] (fig. 7). The song is different from both the formulaic numbers and the use of song for dark humor in that it is tenuously grounded in the diegesis as though its sole purpose is to represent the doll in a different light. Shorn of orchestral embellishments, the song's lyrics are rendered prominent and they reveal a philosophical theme:

Figure 7 (detail)

Refrain: Both you and I are dolls.
If you think about it, everything is a doll.
  [Repeat twice]

In a mother's lap, the child is the doll;
In the presence of a leader, his devotees are dolls.
The God that resides in the temple is also a doll,
And those who worship that doll are also dolls.

Refrain.

In the hands of the powerful even the good-hearted
  is a doll.
For the haves the have-nots are dolls. [Repeat twice]
The man who works day and night is a doll.
And the man who wanders in suffering is also a doll.

Refrain.

In the hands of fate, all lives are dolls.
In the raging storm, the whole world is a doll;

In the banks of a holy river, virtue becomes a doll,
And as death approaches, life itself is a doll.

Refrain.

In the hands of love, we are all dolls.
Under temptation, intelligence becomes a doll.
In a garden of pleasure, nature is a doll.
In nature's creation, everything is a doll.[37]

The image of the doll in this sequence is intercut with shots of the vagrant, nature, the temple, the dog, and Mallika and Anandan who pass by the singing vagrant. The dirge-like melody and the lyrical transformation of the doll as a metaphor for the vulnerable and the exploited introduce a sober meaning that is at odds with the adventurous form of the narrative. The vagrant's worldview, as inspired by the doll, is comparable to both *Sabotage* and Conrad's text in that it describes human and worldly relationships somewhat reductively as a hive of instrumental interdependence. We see this in the various rungs of intentional and subtle manipulation that extend from the anarchist overlords of Verloc and the Professor, Verloc and the Professor's respective families, Spencer and the Verloc family, Scotland Yard and Spencer, and even Mrs. Verloc's marriage of convenience to Mr. Verloc.

While there are very few sermonizing moments such as these in Hitchcock's films, I would venture to include Norman Bates's metaphor of private traps in *Psycho* (1960) and to a lesser degree Uncle Charlie's vicious rant on city women in *Shadow of a Doubt* as instances in which statements by deranged characters express a cynical perspective on society. Similarly, the lyrics also provide another clue for comprehending Balachander's interest in the suspense-mystery genres as vehicles for articulating a grim vision of human nature. And finally, as a commentary on manipulation, the lyrics illuminate both Balachander and Hitchcock's exertion of artistic control as orchestrators of suspense and the *deus ex machina*. Perhaps the most striking irony of the song is that at its end, the vagrant singer's own puppet-like station in the narrative is asserted by the punitive *deus ex machina* that kills him off in the car accident. In that regard, as another surrogate of Stevie, the vagrant's death illustrates the indistinguishability of preying and playing both as film form and theme.

Conclusion: The Two Hitchcocks

Sabotage lends itself to the idioms of Indian melodrama in that its principal focus is on the sacrifice and suffering borne by Mrs.Verloc as a consequence of her uncaring husband's actions. Indeed, our heightened response to the bomb sequence is in many ways a reflection of the violation of that familial unit. The American title for the film, *A Woman Alone*, explicitly invites us to consider Mrs. Verloc as the protagonist of the film and places the film under the subgenre of the "woman's film." Like Indian cinema, in which symbolic relationships, as Allen notes, are often literally translated into familial bonds, in *Sabotage* too "the family is somehow always present, even in the abstract social and public space of the modern world."[38] A typical Indian adaptation of *Sabotage* would have emphasized the family plot and portrayed the pairing of Mrs. Verloc with Sargent Spencer either as a progressive ending or as an unfulfilled romance. Arguably, an Indian adaptation would have also redeemed Verloc himself. Such an adaptation would privilege Hitchcock as the auteur of the sober melodramatic content in *Sabotage* rather than the master and player of suspense.

While Balachander rescues Stevie in his version, it is significant that he achieves that redemption through an indifference to the element that is most salient in Indian cinema: the extraordinary reliance on character-driven drama. In doing so, he honors the playful Hitchcock over Hitchcock the dramatist, who frequently described his suspenseful plots and adventurous narratives as secondary to romantic concerns. Accordingly, by correctly identifying and exploiting the motif of deception that is at the heart of the suspenseful, semi-playful Stevie sequence, Balachander fulfills Hitchcock's own desire to make a suspense film, a situational thriller within a "looser film" not bound by characters.[39] One could argue that as a result Balachander's characters lack depth and that the film is considerably different from his other works, in which moral ambiguity is complexly conveyed through the antihero protagonist. But even here, one could read the duplicitous constitution of the doll/bomb as an inanimate avatar of the Hitchcockian villain and ambiguous identification as displaced to the spectator's desire to witness a thrilling onscreen explosion. Moreover, in a remarkable manner, the two-dimensional characterization can be seen as contributing to a lighter interpretation of the theme in Conrad's text and *Sabotage* as put forth by Leitch: the absence of a "purposive, rational, individual action."[40] As I have shown, that absence leads to a different conclusion in *Bommai*. For in replacing the agency of characters with the Hitchcockian game of safe-suspense, adventure, *deus ex machina*, and teasing equivocation (doll/bomb), Balachander declares that it is the ludic Hitchcock who aids him in the redemption of Stevie and in imagining a sportive alternative to the bomb-plot in *Sabotage*.

Notes

My thanks to Sidney Gottlieb and Richard Allen for their numerous editorial comments and guidance.

1. See essays by Richard Allen, Priyadarshini Shanker, and Richard Ness in "Hitchcock and Hindi Cinema: A Dossier," *Hitchcock Annual* 15 (2006), 173-241.

2. Devika Bai, "The Indian Hitchcock," *The New Straits Times*, April 15, 2014, online at http://www2.nst.com.my/nation/the-indian-hitchcock-1.566954. See also http://www.statemaster.com/encyclopedia/S.-Balachander.

3. Vikram Sampath, *Voice of the Veena: S.Balachander* (New Delhi: Rain Tree, 2012), 355-57.

4. Sampath, "Celluloid Magic," in *Voice of the Veena: S. Balachander* (New Delhi: Rain Tree, 2012), 86-87.

5. Sampath, "Celluloid Magic," 61-62.

6. Sampath, "A Genius is Born," 16.

7. Raymond Smullyan is the most popular composer of chess-problems within the detective fiction format; see his *The Chess Mysteries of Sherlock Holmes: Fifty Tantalizing Problems of Chess Detection* (New York: Dover Publications, 1974), xii.

8. Sampath, "The Man and the Musician," 350; "Select letters written by Balachander to his family members while on concert tours" (Appendix 7), in Sampath, *Voice of the Veena: S. Balachander*, 426-29.

9. Thomas M. Leitch, *Find the Director and Other Hitchcock Games* (Athens: University of Georgia Press, 1991), 16.

10. Sampath, "On creating a unique style," 147-9.

11. Ashish Rajadhyaksha and Paul Willemen, eds., *Encyclopedia of Indian Cinema*, revised edition (London: Oxford University Press, 1999), 51.

12. See See http://www.ebay.com/itm/ALFRED-HITCHCOCK-SABOTAGE-Sylvia-Sidney-RARE-POSTER-INDIA-NFDC-original-/400967551863.

13. Susan Smith, *Hitchcock: Suspense, Humor, and Tone* (London: British Film Institute, 2000), 7-9.

14. Paula Marantz Cohen, *Alfred Hitchcock: The Legacy of Victorianism* (Lexington: University Press of Kentucky, 1995), 33.

15. Dolls as deceptive tools are featured in Hitchcock's *North by Northwest* (1959), where the exotic figurine contains the microfilm, and more interestingly as a memento of guilt in *Stage Fright* (1950).

16. Alfred Hitchcock, "The Enjoyment of Fear," in *Hitchcock on Hitchcock: Selected Writings and Interviews*, ed. Sidney Gottlieb (Berkeley and Los Angeles: University of California Press, 1995), 116-21.

17. Hitchcock, "The Enjoyment of Fear," 121.

18. Hitchcock, "Core of the Movie—The Chase: An Interview with David Brady," in *Hitchcock on Hitchcock*, 125.

19. Leitch, *Find the Director and Other Hitchcock Games*, 178-79.

20. Hitchcock, "Lecture at Columbia University," in *Hitchcock on Hitchcock*, 273.

21. My thanks to Sidney Gottlieb for alerting me to the relevance of "Bang! You're Dead" to my analysis.

22. Hitchcock, "Core of the Movie – The Chase," in *Hitchcock on Hitchcock*, 125.

23. François Truffaut, *Hitchcock* (New York: Simon and Schuster, 1983), 320. I am grateful to Richard Allen for pointing this out to me.

24. Truffaut, *Hitchcock*, 73.

25. Leitch, *Find the Director and Other Hitchcock Games*, 19.

26. Smith, *Hitchcock: Suspense, Humor, and Tone*, 23.

27. Smith, *Hitchcock: Suspense, Humor, and Tone*, 19-20.

28. Smith, *Hitchcock: Suspense, Humor, and Tone*, 32-33.

29. John W. Roberts, "From Hidden Pictures to Productive Pictures: Hitchcock's Ludic Style," *Hitchcock Annual* 19 (2014): 196-97.

30. Smith, *Hitchcock: Suspense, Humor, and Tone*, 12.

31. Truffaut, *Hitchcock*, 138.

32. Richard Allen, "Narrative Form," in *Hitchcock's Romantic Irony* (New York: Columbia University Press, 2007), 37, 39.

33. Leitch, *Find the Director and Other Hitchcock Games*, 76, 100.

34. Avrom Fleishman, "*The Secret Agent* Sabotaged?" in *Conrad on Film*, ed. Gene M. Moore (Cambridge: Cambridge University Press, 1997), 53.

35. Smith, *Hitchcock: Suspense, Humor, and Tone*, 32.

36. Shalini Shah, "The Bulbul Still Sings," *The Hindu*, August 31, 2009, online at http://www.thehindu.com/todays-paper/tp-features/tp-metroplus/the-bulbul-still-sings/article637509.ece.

37. I am grateful to Dr. Rajalakshmi Radhakrishnan and Dr. Lalitha John for their translation of the lyrics.

38. Richard Allen, "To Catch a Jewel Thief," *Hitchcock Annual* 15 (2006): 239.

39. Agreeing with Truffaut's distinction between situation-based and character-based films, Hitchcock says, "I've often wondered whether I could do a suspense story within a looser film, in a form that's not so tight." Truffaut, *Hitchcock*, 315.

40. Thomas Leitch, "Murderous Victims in *The Secret Agent* and *Sabotage*," *Literature/Film Quarterly* 14, no. 1 (1986): 65.

JANET BERGSTROM

Hitchcock/Truffaut, *the Movie:*
The Latest Version of a Legend

Legends are kept alive by variants introduced by different tellers, depending on their needs or perspectives. Kent Jones's 2015 documentary, *Hitchcock/Truffaut*, is the most recent presentation of the creation and influence of François Truffaut's famous book based on a week of audiotaped interviews that the young French director carried out with Alfred Hitchcock in Hollywood in August 1962.[1] Hitchcock was then in the midst of post-production for *The Birds*.

First published in French in 1966 as *Le cinéma selon Hitchcock* and in English the next year as *Hitchcock*, it has subsequently been published in many languages and has never gone out of print in French or English.[2] Since then a mountain of books on Hitchcock has appeared, but this one remains special. It can be read for pleasure and inspiration by anyone, whether a professional or a child lucky enough to have a "movie buff" parent hand it to him or her to encourage a desire to make films. That's how David Fincher got the book as a boy and started reading it over and over, as he tells us in this documentary. After all these years, Truffaut's *Hitchcock* has not only remained *the* essential book on Hitchcock, it is one of the best loved and most frequently quoted books on the cinema, period.

Although the documentary keeps that title, in this version of the legend, the book leaves center stage fairly quickly. It acts as a springboard into the seductive world of Hitchcock's films, their ambiance, shots, and materiality, in a different way than Hitchcock's descriptions of scenes or his rationale for shot sequencing and larger strategies as found in the book or, even more so, in the un-edited audio interview.[3] It seems that Truffaut's was the first interview book to be entirely devoted to a film director. We know from his correspondence that he had to fight to persuade his publishers that his project was not too technical to appeal to a general audience. His correspondence also lets us see how much time and effort he devoted to locating film prints and having frame enlargements made to illustrate Hitchcock's statements as precisely as possible. And he had to keep insisting that images should appear at the point in the text where they were discussed rather than being grouped in a separate section of the book, which was the typical, less costly practice at the time. All this work on the iconography and page layout was part of Truffaut's overall strategy to convince the public, in the U.S. and in France, that Hitchcock was a film artist, not simply a commercially successful entertainer, a persona that Hitchcock himself seemed to relish in humorously macabre appearances on the screen in theatrical trailers advertising his films and in his introductions to the very popular *Alfred Hitchcock Presents* television series. Truffaut often decided to sacrifice text, over the months and months of revisions, to give more space to the images.

Kent Jones did not attempt to transpose the book (text and iconography) into audio-visual form. He continued Truffaut's objectives through a series of brilliantly selected moments from Hitchcock's films, often only part of a shot with subtle gradations of lighting, position, or movement, especially changes in facial expression, and through the occasional sound of Hitchcock's well-known voice. Jones's choice of film clips was inspired and inspiring, with important credit due, one assumes, to his editor Rachel Reichman. These moments from Hitchcock's films demonstrate his undying achievements as a visual stylist (most of them are wordless), furthering Truffaut's mission as expressed in the letter he had written to Hitchcock to persuade him to take part in this enterprise: "If, overnight, the cinema had to do without a sound track and become once again a silent art, then many directors would be forced into unemployment, but, among the survivors, there would be Alfred Hitchcock and everyone would realize at last that he is the greatest film director in the world."[4]

Structure

Truffaut planned to organize his book chronologically: a sketch of Hitchcock's early life would be followed by a discussion of all of his films, one by one. That approach would allow Hitchcock to demonstrate his increasing mastery as a director as he went along and to explain innovations from his own perspective. And indeed, Hitchcock seized the opportunity to describe, often with growing excitement, how he had come upon new ways of "making the point visually," of using sound, and of focalizing stories psychologically. The "master of suspense," as he was known, had many other things he felt it was important to talk about in response to his interlocutor. He often illustrated how he found a solution to a particular problem by describing a particular scene shot by shot, sound by sound (for *Blackmail* and after). The chronological approach made it evident what a large, complex, and coherent body of work the director had created.

The interview didn't always move ahead in an orderly fashion. Hitchcock thought that *The Birds* would be finished by the time Truffaut arrived with his translator and indispensable assistant, Helen Scott.[5] Instead, he was in the midst of carrying out his epoch-making decision to substitute electronic sound for music for the entire soundtrack, working with collaborators in Germany, Remi Gassman and Oskar Salas, using the Mixtur-Trautonium.[6] Sometimes the group went from a screening of the latest version of the film to the recording room for the interview. It was hardly surprising that Hitchcock kept returning to *The Birds* throughout the discussion. Later, Truffaut and Helen Scott, who became co-editor during the complicated four-year book production process, decided to restructure the text of the interview, not only to tame *The Birds*, but to augment parts of it they thought were sketchy, such as Hitchcock's background and early career.

Truffaut originally believed that the book could be published very quickly in both French and English. As he wrote to Helen Scott on July 5, 1962, "I realize now that our bilingual recording method will enormously facilitate publication since, as soon as the tapes have been transcribed, we will have a book in two languages requiring practically no translation (simply a scrupulous revision of the French text)."[7] Complications surrounding the book's production and transformation from 1962 to 1966, such as multiple copy-editors working in two languages, resulted in a condensed and often re-worded version of the original interview, replacing Hitchcock's vivid, idiomatic way of explaining what he was doing with flat, standard English.[8] Compared to the audio interview, Truffaut omitted a great deal of context because of lack of space and perhaps for other reasons: among the kinds of things left out were most collaborators, technical details, production facilities, industry personnel, and crisscrossing filiations that Hitchcock explained to show how his British career was connected with his later one.

Jones took this elimination of information to an extreme. He dispensed entirely with the contextualization that did make it into Truffaut's book. The progression of Hitchcock's work over time was not what Jones was after. He included virtually nothing about collaborators (aside from a few actors), production conditions, technical innovations, or context of any kind. This is unfortunate, especially since today, unlike when Truffaut's book appeared, no one needs to be persuaded of Hitchcock's importance—that is, no one who has been exposed to his films. And unless Jones intended to preach to the choir, as the saying goes, an expanded audience for Hitchcock could use some information. Among the things we learn from the book that did not make it into the documentary was that Hitchcock emphasized how he studied films and trade journals beginning at a young age, long before he began to work in the industry.

During the August 1962 sessions, 52 half-hour reel-to-reel tapes were recorded, or about 26 hours of interview.[9] Copies of those tapes at the Margaret Herrick Library in Beverly Hills have been consulted and quoted by scholars for years. Jones mentioned in radio interviews that he had access to another set of the tapes held in Truffaut's archives in Paris. Even more readily accessible, although edited, are about 11 hours of the interview that was broadcast on French radio and can be readily found on the internet.[10] It is striking, considering all the audio material available to Jones, how infrequently we hear Hitchcock's voice in his film. We are not treated to even one of Hitchcock's lively shot-by-shot, sound-by-sound descriptions that show so well how he had found the best way to achieve his objectives, or, in other words, how he was becoming exactly what Truffaut had set out to prove, a master of *mise-en-scène*. Truffaut voice is given more prominence in Jones's film than in the book or in the original tapes. Only occasionally do we hear Helen Scott's simultaneous translations.

Unlike Truffaut's care in guiding the reader toward understanding how Hitchcock developed in more or less linear fashion, Jones not only mixes up the order of the film extracts, he doesn't even identify them except on rare occasions when, for instance, a poster for a movie may lead to a clip. Anyone inspired by an extract from a Hitchcock film who doesn't know what it is will not know how to find it later. Probably Jones's top tier audience consists of Hitchcock aficionados like himself, who would be happy to be immersed in the Hitchcock universe. But considering the commentators he chose—all of them film directors—Jones must also have wanted to inspire new generations of aspiring filmmakers. Given his care and expertise in the art of audience-building in his varied professional roles, perhaps he could provide a key to the film extracts in an extension of his documentary on the internet.

After some quick, key moments from famous films (if you know them) intercut with Jones's opening title cards, he begins his documentary with one of the most brilliant sequences in visual storytelling in Hitchcock's career—a stunning series of shots without dialogue from the dinner table scene in *Sabotage*, building to the instant when Verloc (Oscar Homolka) realizes that his wife (Sylvia Sidney), hesitating as she holds the carving knife, may try to kill him, in reaction to her little brother's death that day when a time-bomb exploded that was inside a box Verloc asked the boy to deliver. Concentrating on those shots out of context has a magical effect, as if never before had they received due attention: you can focus entirely on how intricately conceived the sequence is, with many incremental movements in each shot, changes in camera angle and shot scale, the facial expressiveness of two exceptional actors, and, in the last shot we see, the camera moving with Homolka as he slowly rises from his chair and comes very close to it, the background by then almost completely out of focus. The complexity of the shot development is impossible to reproduce through frame enlargements because each shot has so many variations within it. Truffaut did his best in the double-page spread that David Fincher calls our attention to.[11] For Jones to open with this shot sequence, and to stop where he did was a superb way to convince anyone that Hitchcock was no ordinary director and that he had a psychological sensibility that was not easy to comprehend. Visually, he was a master.

At the point Jones ends the scene in *Sabotage* there is no telling what will happen and how strangely the rest of the scene will unfold, shot by shot. (Later in the documentary, Jones shows us part of what leads to this extract and part of what follows.) We couldn't see these shots in the same way if they had not been isolated from their place in the film as a whole; their power would fade in memory, probably overridden by the scene's dramatic climax (a murder). If one thought about it at all, one might have the impression that what preceded the murder was straightforward preparation for it. This is not unlike what Raymond Bellour analyzed long ago in an apparently small transitional scene from *The Big Sleep*: why were twelve shots needed, when memory more likely recalled only a few?[12]

The first words we hear in Jones's documentary are spoken by Hitchcock, mid-way though the *Sabotage* sequence just described, followed by Truffaut:

Hitchcock: Why do these Hitchcock films stand up well? They don't look old-fashioned. Well I don't know the answer.
Truffaut: Perhaps because they are so rigorous. They're not tied to a particular time either, because they're made only in relation to you, yourself.

This exchange is not in the book. Moreover, the voice of Helen Scott, their interpreter, was erased from the audio, giving the impression that the two men are speaking to each other directly, without an intermediary, one in English and the other in French. Even though Hitchcock scholars know that many changes were made to Hitchcock's statements as he spoke them in the interview compared to what was printed in the book, the viewer of this film probably assumes that everything we hear Hitchcock say, in off-screen voice-over, is in the book that is its subject.

The Commentators

In Jones's documentary we move forward more or less thematically through thoughtful statements from ten on-screen commentators, all of them male filmmakers, mostly mid-career: Wes Anderson, Olivier Assayas, Peter Bogdanovich, Arnaud Desplechin, David Fincher, James Gray, Kiyoshi Kurosawa, Richard Linklater, Paul Schrader, and Martin Scorsese. (No critics or historians are mentioned, much less seen.) Their observations cue or sometimes follow clips from Hitchcock's films, in no particular order and almost always without being identified—until we get to long sections on *Vertigo* and *Psycho*. Kent Jones, who would make an excellent commentator himself, chose not to appear on-camera or in the spare voice-over narration. Bogdanovich, Schrader, and Scorsese add depth by taking a historical view, recalling the lack of critical respect, if not disdain, for Hitchcock initially and how that changed, partly because of the Hitchcock/Truffaut book, and that Hitchcock progressively became an essential point of reference for filmmakers like themselves.

Early on, a number of the commentators talk about the book briefly; later, they mostly talk about Hitchcock. David Fincher speaks at some length about *Sabotage*. He appears on the screen immediately after we see the dinner table scene described above, implicitly identifying that film after the fact:

> That was incredibly fascinating to me that these two
> people from very different worlds who were both doing
> the same job, how they would talk about . . . He talks

about things, contextualizing what the work of the director truly is at its most fundamental and most simple.

Other examples from this introductory section give a sense of the director speaking as well as the book:

Paul Schrader: There were starting to be these kinds of erudite conversations about the art form. But Truffaut was the first one where you really felt that they were really talking about the craft of it.

Peter Bogdanovich: I think it conclusively changed people's opinions about Hitchcock and so Hitchcock began to be taken much more seriously.

Martin Scorsese: [In terms of what the critical establishment thought serious cinema was,] it was really revolutionary. . . . It was almost as if somebody had taken a weight off our shoulders and said, yes, we can embrace this, we can go.

Very soon the directors talk mostly about Hitchcock, showing different perspectives, as in these examples:

Wes Anderson: He was also conceptual with the way he approached many of these films. This movie I have an idea for a way that I've never worked before. This is somebody whose mind is racing, filled with ideas, and that's why, you know, we refer to him all the time.

David Fincher: If you think that you can hide what your interests are, what your prurient interests are, what your noble interests are, what your fascinations are . . . if you think you can hide that in your work as a film director, you're nuts.

Martin Scorsese: *Vertigo*: I can't really say that I believe the plot. I don't take any of the story seriously, I mean as a realistic story. The plot is just a line that you can hang things on. And the things that he hangs on it are all aspects of cinema poetry.... I can't really tell where things start and end, and I don't care.

Paul Schrader: [Commenting on Kim Novak as the star of *Vertigo*, replacing Vera Miles who had become pregnant] I don't think he would have been able to take Vera Miles into that Judy place.

Olivier Assayas: Hitchcock's genius is based on eroticism, on relatively disturbing emotions. What is surprising and admirable is how he succeeded in communicating these delicate and dark obsessions in a way that was acceptable to all audiences.

Scorsese analyzes some of Hitchcock's techniques, a subject that I wish others had been drawn to (or perhaps that had been included), especially the effect of camera placement for certain shots (in *Psycho*, for instance), alternative placements he could imagine, and why he believed Hitchcock's choice was best for what he wanted to accomplish. Discussing a close shot of the guilty man in *Topaz*, Scorsese comments: "The camera is sort of up above him a little bit. And you see his eyes shift, the eye is not covered, that means the angle has to be just right. And you know he's lying." He discusses *The Wrong Man*, a film he has studied, in appreciative detail, for instance pointing out stylistic choices in the scene after Manny Balestrero (Henry Fonda) has been put into a jail cell:

Those extraordinary inserts, when Henry Fonda is just sitting on the bunk. He looks at the cell around him and [Hitchcock] cuts to different sections of the cell. What makes you feel oppressed? The lock on the door? From what angle? Is it really his point of view? All these things are remarkable, I think.

The documentary sketches the backgrounds of Truffaut and Hitchcock through fleeting glimpses of well-travelled territory. For Truffaut, we get a little about how the interview was set up and its mechanics; he and fellow critics at the *Cahiers du Cinéma* when they championed auteurs like Hitchcock; father figures (Bazin, Renoir, Rossellini, Hitchcock); and sequences from *The 400 Blows* that Truffaut and Hitchcock discussed in the interview. Jones expands the scope of his film beyond the book to highlight Truffaut, although not in depth. Toward this end, Jones found a perceptive commentator in director and former *Cahiers du Cinéma* editor Olivier Assayas:

> It's not just that Truffaut wrote a book about Hitchcock, the book is an essential part of his work. Truffaut isn't a stylist. He shoots beautifully, but that's never the point. If there's one thing he learned from Hitchcock, it's concision, speed. But the difference is that Hitchcock has an absolutely mathematical sense of construction of his sequences. Hitchcock is a theoretician of space.

Brief, familiar references are made to some of Hitchcock's background, including bits of home movies showing his wife and working partner Alma; Hitchcock playing with his toddler Patricia; and his move to Hollywood via agreements with Selznick International Pictures (you need to pause the film to look at the documents flying by, but we can see that Hitchcock was getting pay increases, meaning success). Jones returns to the lives of both men at the end of his film.

The main part is loosely devoted to topics that generations of Hitchcock scholars, critics, filmmakers, and unclassifiable individuals, mushrooming in our age of bloggers, have never stopped discussing, among them: "your casual approach to plausibility"; suspense and surprise; the use of space in the frame; the expansion and contraction of time; working with actors; falling from great heights; spirituality; dream logic, leading to a fascinating homage to *Vertigo* that is especially strong on the parts with non-realistic colored tinting; and "the public," leading to a multi-faceted section on *Psycho*. In the film, these themes are usually accompanied by excellent film extracts and remarks by Jones's commentators.

Several sections seem to present an implicit argument showing that Hitchcock was actively involved on the set as his films were being shot, as film historian Bill Krohn has documented most thoroughly, countering the commonplace view that for Hitchcock shooting was boring, as the director himself often stated, because he already had the finished film in his head by then.[13] We see on the screen briefly a partial view of a typed document about *The Birds* called "Mr. Hitchcock's Notes/Background," with phrases highlighted presumably (not explicitly) to indicate Hitchcock's detailed involvement beyond the script stage, and we see photos of Hitchcock on the set of various films, probably for the same unstated reason. A long section on Hitchcock and actors speaks to the same issue—his active involvement during shooting—as he explains (through voice-over) how he handled two specific scenes: directing Montgomery Clift, over the actor's objections, to look in a particular direction in *I Confess*, and Cary Grant and Ingrid Bergman's famously endless kiss in *Notorious*, as we see perfectly chosen film extracts on screen. It is curious that Jones did not choose to make this point directly, if that was the point he wanted to make.

The kiss in *Notorious* also serves as the fulcrum for one of Jones's most thought-provoking commentators, Kiyoshi Kurosawa:

> Thanks to Hollywood, he could really become Alfred Hitchcock. And thanks to Alfred Hitchcock, the American cinema that I dream of renewed itself. One must be very careful. So special, so unique, he portrayed himself as a mainstream figure, and even though many of his films were popular, when you consider him as a filmmaker, he's really at the furthest edge of things. What he says in *Hitchcock/Truffaut* resonates for me as a filmmaker. It's the attitude I

think I should have when I'm making my own films. It's almost as if it were a Bible. But at the same time, I have strictly forbidden myself to try to imitate him. In *Notorious*, the famous kiss is a perfectly demonic shot, no matter how many times you watch it. The whole time he's staying on their faces, and you don't know what's going on with their bodies.

Toward the end of the documentary, we see: Philippe Halsman's photographs of the interview group; Hitchcock and Truffaut continuing their correspondence and friendship after the interview; and Truffaut, looking like a statesman, presenting Hitchcock with the AFI Lifetime Achievement Award on March 7, 1979 (this information is imprinted on the film clip). The award ceremony is a sad piece to have included because Hitchcock looks barely cognizant, unable or unwilling to rise to the occasion. The director ought to have received this award earlier in his life, when he might have accepted it with brio. Here, he simply does not look well. Nothing about this is mentioned by the narrator. Next we see the notification for the memorial mass for Hitchcock after he passed away about a year later. References to Truffaut's life conclude with images of the director in his prime, as we hear of his untimely death four years after Hitchcock's, at the age of fifty-two. The revised edition of the Hitchcock/Truffaut book, we are told, was his last completed project, "published a few months before he died."

Jones adds an epilogue showing the famous scene in *Notorious* in which Alicia Huberman (Ingrid Bergman) hides a key from her husband, Alexander Sebastian (Claude Rains), in their bedroom before going downstairs to meet their guests. Then one of Hitchcock's most famous overhead crane shots starts very high and slowly moves down to a crowded party in their home, ending on a close shot of Bergman's hand held behind her back that opens to show the key she still holds. That is the last moment of Kent Jones's film.

In the book, Hitchcock had something to say about the reason for that elaborate camera movement, combining film technique with a dramatic rationale as he so often did in his explanations:

> There again we've substituted the language of the camera for dialogue. In *Notorious* that sweeping movement of the camera is making a statement. What it's saying is: "There's a large reception being held in this house, but there is a drama here which no one is aware of, and at the core of that drama is this tiny object, this key."[14]

In the book, Truffaut tells Hitchcock, "In my opinion, *Notorious* is the very quintessence of Hitchcock," and is eager to lay out his reasons for this and to hear Hitchcock's reaction.[15] This is one of the few times in the text and in the oral interview when Truffaut speaks at length, explaining clearly his reasons for valuing Hitchcock's films so highly and especially this one. In the documentary, as we watch *Notorious*, we hear only the very ending of Truffaut's explanation to Hitchcock without mentioning the film by name:

> *Truffaut*: In nine out of ten of your films you show characters divided by a secret that they refuse to reveal to one another. The atmosphere becomes more and more oppressive until finally they decide to open up and thus liberate themselves. Does this ring true for you?
> *Hitchcock*: Sure.
> *Truffaut*: In the end, you are mostly interested in filming moral dilemmas within the framework of the crime story.
> *Hitchcock*: Sure, that's right.
> *Truffaut*: So, that's my conclusion.

That makes for a neat ending to the film, but it does not do justice to the encounter from Truffaut's point of view. He has taken pains to explain himself—one senses that he prepared exactly what he wanted to say—and Hitchcock agrees with him. However, Hitchcock replies in monosyllables, as he often does when affirmation may really mean that he wants to move on. He may or may not be in full agreement.

Finessing

Not everything is quite what it might appear to be. Omitting most of Truffaut's analysis of *Notorious* that he had the courage to tell its director face to face, something very important to Truffaut, amounts to finessing the original material. That sort of thing makes itself felt in other ways throughout Jones's film.

There is an apparently small error of fact near the beginning that could have opened onto an interesting area, had the director been inclined to bring the history of the interview into his film. Jones's narrator mistakenly tells us that Hitchcock "has just completed his fortieth feature, *The Birds*." Precisely because Hitchcock was not finished, Truffaut had the good fortune to come upon the director at a point when all the details were still fresh in his mind, details that he talked about during the interview: difficulties he had overcome, challenges ahead in order to achieve the effects he wanted. But because the book was not published until four years later, everything related to *The Birds* had to be put in the past tense. Many of Hitchcock's statements were omitted (including almost all of the valuable in-progress production information), other things he said were condensed, and almost everything that remained was paraphrased in a way that cut his excitement at the experimentations he was engaged in.

Another example of finessing occurs when Arnaud Desplechin brings up the familiar theme of the transference of guilt in Hitchcock's films. He forgets to mention Claude Chabrol and Eric Rohmer, who stated in 1957, in the first book written on Hitchcock, that the transfer of guilt is one of the chief characteristics of Hitchcock's work, in its moral dimension. They already called it "the famous transference of guilt."[16]

One of Jones's thematic strategies is to highlight phrases from the book out of context: the rest of the page is darkened and cannot be read. My favorite example is "impression of the fear" because it is so suggestive of the ambiance Hitchcock excelled in creating in myriad ways. But Hitchcock did not speak those words in the section of the recorded interview corresponding to its place in the book version; I would like to think that he spoke it in another interview and that the editors imported it rather than that they invented it. Hitchcock is talking about *The Birds*. In the book he states:

> When the birds attack the barricaded house and Melanie is cringing back on the sofa, I kept the camera back and used the space to show the nothingness from which she's shrinking. When I went back to her, I varied that by placing the camera high to convey the impression of the fear that rising in her.[17]

In the audio interview, Hitchcock says:

> You may need space, and use it dramatically. For example, in *The Birds*, I deliberately, when the girl shrunk back on the sofa, I kept the camera back and used the space to indicate the nothingness from which she was shrinking, you see. And then I varied that when I went back to her, I went high to get the impression of that thing coming up. [Helen Scott translates this as: "cette chose montait en elle."][18]

There are endless examples of words, phrases, or entire sections of Hitchcock's explanations in the original interview that do not appear in the book or that have been transformed. I am drawing attention to this one because the viewer will assume that the phrase highlighted from the book, "impression of the fear," is in the interview, given that this is a documentary about the interview book.

A different kind of finessing is exemplified in the creative editing of statements that Hitchcock made in the interview and that were published in the book in close to identical form. For instance, Jones uses two non-contiguous statements as if

Figure 1   Figure 2

they followed each other from one of Hitchcock's longer explanations in the book where he refers to something he learned in art school: "There's no such thing as a face; it's non-existent until the light hits it. And there's no such thing as a line. It's just light and shade."[19] As we hear the second of these pronouncements, we see two striking images from *Blackmail* (figures 1 and 2). The effect is excellent, but these images come from Jones, not Truffaut: the discussion in the book, at that point, is primarily devoted to *Rope*. The relationship between the Hitchcock/Truffaut book and this film is not simple.

Everyone Wants to Talk About Hitchcock

Reactions to Jones's film show boundless enthusiasm for Hitchcock. All kinds of written and radio interviews with the director have made that palpable, especially spontaneous comments from callers at the end of radio programs. Not only has *Vertigo* displaced *Citizen Kane* as the number one movie of all time—a far cry from reactions to it when it was released— but more and more Hitchcock, potentially all of Hitchcock, is becoming a shared point of reference and pleasure. In this film, Jones used the Hitchcock/Truffaut book as a stepping stone to display a fascinating selection of Hitchcock moments. And sometimes his commentators sparked interest in their own way of thinking and in their own work as filmmakers because of what they said about Hitchcock.

Diverging from the classic book, Jones did not follow Truffaut's choices in text or iconography or the form of

Hitchcock's explanations. He highlighted Truffaut in a way that went beyond the book entirely yet that remained sketchy and at the level of fairly well-known information. On the other hand, his selections from the audio interview gave the impression that Truffaut was more of an equal partner in the discussion than he was. Truffaut's impressive preparations were meant to draw out Hitchcock for this book-length interview. Only occasionally did he offer a sustained statement about something that he was eager to hear Hitchcock react to—such as the way he had shot a scene in *The 400 Blows* (documented in Jones's film) or his analysis of *Notorious*.

I only hope that, in the interest of informed audience-building, the Hitchcock cognoscenti will continue to help everyone understand more, not less, of the complexity of the film and television environments during the times in which Hitchcock moved forward, as he himself felt it necessary to start to explain given the opportunity that Truffaut had offered him. Perhaps one of the lessons of Jones's documentary is that an equally appealing film could be made that would convey a great deal of information beyond that which is quickly digestible, that would repay repeated viewings. It would be worth it to find champions within the current documentary sphere who could use the kinds of visuals that Kent Jones knew how to choose so well and draw on the same, rich Hitchcock/Truffaut interview to illustrate and analyze Hitchcock's precise ways of explaining his reasons for scene construction (and film construction) that does not forget context and that does not separate drama (or art) from technology.

Notes

1. *Hitchcock/Truffaut*, directed by Kent Jones, written by Kent Jones and Serge Toubiana, edited by Rachel Reichman, narrated by Bob Balaban, original music composed by Jeremiah Bornfield, produced by Charles S. Cohen and Olivier Mille, Artline Films/Cohen Media Group/ARTE, France, 2015, 80 minutes.

2. François Truffaut, with the collaboration of Helen Scott, *Le Cinéma selon Hitchcock* (Paris: Robert Laffont, 1966); François Truffaut, with the collaboration of Helen G. Scott, *Hitchcock* (New York: Simon and Schuster, 1967).

3. In 1984, Patricia Hitchcock O'Connell donated a complete set of the tapes of the August 1962 interview as part of the Hitchcock Collection to the Margaret Herrick Library, Academy of Motion Pictures Arts and Sciences, Beverly Hills.

4. François Truffaut, *Letters*, ed. Gilles Jacob and Claude de Givray, trans. and ed. Gilbert Adair (London: Faber and Faber, 1989), 179.

5. Helen Scott was more than Truffaut's translator and assistant. Born in New York and raised in Paris, she had to leave France in 1943 because she was Jewish. She went to Brazzaville, Congo, where she made radio broadcasts for the Free French. After the war, she was press attaché for Chief Justice Robert Jackson at the Nuremberg trials, became a senior editor at the United Nations, and then director of public relations for the French Film Office in the U.S. In that role, she had been instrumental in helping the French New Wave—and Truffaut in particular, ever since his first feature, *The 400 Blows*—become known to the American press. See Serge Toubiana, "Helen G. Scott, l'intrépide," *Cahiers du Cinéma* 402 (December 1978), xvi.

6. The credits for *The Birds* list Hitchcock's longtime composer, Bernard Herrmann, as "Sound Consultant." Remi Gassman and Oskar Salas are credited for "Composition and Production of Electronic Sound."

7. Truffaut, *Letters*, 191.

8. Differences between the audio interview and the text of the book are the subject of my essay "Lost in Translation? Listening to the Hitchcock-Truffaut Interview," in *A Companion to Alfred Hitchcock*, ed. Thomas Leitch and Leland Poague (Malden, MA: Wiley-Blackwell, 2011), 387-404. I drew on documentation in the Hitchcock Collection at the Margaret Herrick Library, the Truffaut Collection at the library of the Cinémathèque Française (then known as the Bibliothèque du Film), and published correspondence to trace the long history of the book's production in French and English, and provided examples of strong differences between Hitchcock's words as spoken and as published.

9. See my essay "Lost in Translation" for more information, and also the entry in the Margaret Herrick Library on-line database.

10. Serge Toubiana, co-writer with Jones of the *Hitchcock/Truffaut* film, and Nicolas Saada prepared a selection of 11 hours and 15

minutes from the original tapes for broadcast on the French radio station France Culture in 1999. That series is accessible in numerous locations, including via the Hitchcock Zone, at http://the.hitchcock.zone/ wiki/Alfred_Hitchcock_and_Fran%C3%A7ois_ Truffaut_(Aug/1962).

11. I decided to study the scene myself by recreating the images Truffaut had published, capturing the same frames from a DVD. That proved impossible for two reasons: for one thing, I believe that the shots in the book are out of order, a problem that I don't necessarily attribute to Truffaut; more instructively, in attempting to locate precise matches with images in the book, I could see how much variation, operating on a minute scale, was present within each shot, and from shot to shot. Then I discovered the website 1000 Frames of Hitchcock, through a link at The Hitchcock Zone: http://the.hitchcock.zone/wiki/1000_Frames_of_Hitchcock. This is a gift to Hitchcock lovers. To quote the site's description: "British artist Dave Pattern set out to highlight Hitch's visual genius with his series, which compresses each of Hitchcock's 52 major movies down to a mere 1000 frames. That's about six seconds of running time." The frames are individually downloadable. See 1000 Frames of *Sabotage*, at http://the.hitchcock.zone/wiki/1000_Frames_of_Sabotage_(1936), but don't expect to see all the detail of the sequence there.

12. Raymond Bellour, "The Obvious and the Code," *Screen* 15, no. 4 (winter 1974/75), reprinted in Philip Rosen, ed., *Narrative, Apparatus, Ideology* (New York: Columbia University Press, 1986), 93-100.

13. Bill Krohn, *Hitchcock at Work* (London: Phaidon, 2000).

14. François Truffaut, with the collaboration of Helen G. Scott, *Hitchcock*, rev. ed. (New York: Simon and Schuster, 1984), 116.

15. Truffaut, *Hitchcock*, rev. ed., 167.

16. Claude Chabrol and Eric Rohmer, *Hitchcock* (Paris: Editions Universitaires, 1957), 30; in the English version, see Chabrol and Rohmer, *Hitchcock: The First Forty-Four Films*, trans. Stanley Hochman (New York: Frederick Ungar, 1979), 23.

17. Truffaut, *Hitchcock*, rev. ed., 263.

18. The audio can be found in section 19 of the on-line version: "L'effet contre le réalisme (General Technique)."

19. For the fuller version, see Truffaut, *Hitchcock*, rev. ed., 183.

Index to *Hitchcock Annual*
Volumes 1-20

ARTICLES

Alfred Hitchcock on Music in Films, an interview with Stephen Watts, introduction by Margaret Anne O'Connor, 3 (1994): 149-57.

Alfred Hitchcock: Registrar of Births and Deaths, by David Sterritt, 6 (1997-98): 3-18.

Alfred Hitchcock's Cameo in *Vertigo*, by James M. Vest, 8 (1999-2000): 84-92.

Alfred Hitchcock's Carnival, by Mark M. Hennelly, Jr., 13 (2004-05): 154-88.

Alfred Hitchcock's *Easy Virtue* (1927): A Descriptive Shot List, by Sidney Gottlieb, 2 (1993): 41-95.

Alfred Hitchcock's *The Lodger, A Story of the London Fog* (1926): A Descriptive Shot List, by Charles L.P. Silet, 5 (1996-97): 49-109.

Alfred Hitchcock's *The Manxman* (1929): A Descriptive Shot List, by Richard Ness, 4 (1995-96): 61-116.

Alfred Hitchcock's *Number 17* (1932): A Descriptive Shot List, by Michael Sevastakis, 3 (1994): 76-148.

Alfred Hitchcock's Role in *Elstree Calling*, by James M. Vest, 9 (2000-01): 115-26.

Allen, Richard, Avian Metaphor in *The Birds*, 6 (1997-98): 40-67.

_____, An Interview with Jay Presson Allen, 9 (2000-01): 3-22.

_____, Hitchcock After Bellour, 11 (2002-03): 117-47.

_____, Hitchcock and the Wandering Woman: The Influence of Italian Art Cinema on *The Birds*, 18 (2013): 149-94.

_____, Introduction, Gus Van Sant vs. Alfred Hitchcock: A *Psycho* Dossier, 10 (2001-02): 125-26.

_____, Introduction, Hitchcock and Hindi Cinema: A Dossier, 15 (2006-07): 164-72.

_____, *The Lodger* and the Origins of Hitchcock's Aesthetic, 10 (2001-02): 38-78.

_____, Sir John and the Half-Caste: Identity and Representation in Hitchcock's *Murder!*, 13 (2004-05): 92-126.

_____, To Catch a Jewel Thief: Hitchcock and Indian Modernity, 15 (2006-07): 215-41.

Alma in Wonderland, 15 (2006-07): 35-37.

Ambivalence (*Suspicion*), by Bill Krohn, 11 (2002-03): 67-116.

REVIEWS

Morris, Christopher D., *The Hanging Figure: On Suspense and the Films of Alfred Hitchcock*, rev. by Angelo Restivo, 12 (2003-04): 168-76.

Naremore, James, Hitchcock Now [review of Thomas Leitch and Leland Poague, ed., *A Companion to Alfred Hitchcock*, and David Boyd and R. Barton Palmer, ed., *Hitchcock at the Source: The Auteur as Adapter*], 17 (2011): 195-206.

Naremore, James, *More than Night: Film Noir in Its Contexts*, rev. by Charles L.P. Silet, 8 (1999-2000): 173-75.

_____, *North by Northwest*. Rutgers Films in Print, rev. by Christopher Brookhouse, 4 (1995-96): 164-65.

Ness, Richard, rev. of Camille Paglia, *The Birds*, 8 (1999-2000): 161-65.

Nourmand, Tony and Mark H. Wolff, eds., *Hitchcock Poster Art: From the Mark H. Wolff Collection*, rev. by Charles L.P. Silet, 9 (2000-01): 189-90.

O'Connell, Pat Hitchcock and Laurent Bouzereau, *Alma Hitchcock: The Woman Behind the Man*, rev. by Charles L.P. Silet, 12 (2003-04): 186-90.

O'Connor, Margaret Anne, rev. of Virginia Wright Wexman, *Creating the Couple: Love, Marriage, and Hollywood Performance*, 7 (1998-99): 127-29.

Of Flashbacks and *Femmes Fatales*, by Leland Poague [review of James F. Maxfield, *The Fatal Woman: Sources of Male Anxiety in American Film Noir, 1941-1991*, and E. Ann Kaplan, ed., *Women in Film Noir*, new edition], 8 (1999-2000): 131-55.

Orr, John, *Hitchcock and Twentieth-Century Cinema*, rev. by Thomas Leitch, 14 (2005-06): 196-205.

Paglia, Camille, *The Birds*, rev. by Richard Ness, 8 (1999-2000): 161-65.

Palmer, William J., *The Films of the Eighties: A Social History*, rev. by Frank P. Tomasulo, 3 (1994): 182-94.

Parrish, Virginia, rev. of Walter Raubicheck and Walter Srebnick, eds., *Hitchcock's Rereleased Films: From* Rope *to* Vertigo, 2 (1993): 137-39.

Patalas, Enno, *Alfred Hitchcock*, rev. by James Bade, 12 (2003-04): 191-99.

Perry, Dennis R., *Hitchcock and Poe: The Legacy of Delight and Terror*, rev. by Walter Raubicheck, 12 (2003-04): 177-82.

Contributors

Janet Bergstrom, Professor of Cinema & Media Studies, UCLA, specializes in archivally-based, cross-national studies of émigré directors such as F. W. Murnau, Jean Renoir, Josef von Sternberg, Alfred Hitchcock, and Fritz Lang as well as French or Francophone directors Chantal Akerman and Claire Denis. She has published five documentaries on DVD.

Aparna Frank recently completed her dissertation on the early feature films of avant-garde filmmakers Mani Kaul and Kumar Shahani in the Department of Cinema Studies, New York University. She has an M.A. in cinema studies from New York University as well. She has taught courses on European and American new wave films, film color, and film analysis at New York University and Hunter College. Her research interests include the aesthetic study of film, non-mainstream film practices in India, and histories of modernist and avant-garde cinema.

Paul Haspel, originally from Bethesda, Maryland, received his Ph.D. from the University of Maryland, College Park. Currently an instructor in English at Central Carolina Community College in Sanford, North Carolina, he has published essays on the work of various directors including Stanley Kubrick, John Waters, Clint Eastwood, Paul Mazursky, Gillo Pontecorvo, Barry Levinson, Hal Ashby, Alan J. Pakula, and George Roy Hill. He is presently working on a book about cinematic portrayals of Washington, D.C.

Henry K. Miller is the editor of *The Essential Raymond Durgnat* (BFI/Palgrave Macmillan, 2014) and has been a regular contributor to *Sight and Sound* since 2006. His work has appeared in *Screen* and *Critical Quarterly*, among other journals, and in a number of BFI DVD booklets. He is an affiliate member of the University of Cambridge's Centre for Film and Screen, and an Honorary Research Associate at the Slade School of Fine Art. His research on Hitchcock and C.A.

Lejeune was conducted under the auspices of a postdoctoral fellowship awarded by the Paul Mellon Centre for Studies in British Art in 2014.

Amy Sargeant has written extensively on British Cinema of the silent and sound periods and is especially interested in exchanges between film and other cultural activities and industries. She is author of *British Cinema: A Critical History* (BFI, 2005; second edition forthcoming) and her most recent book is *Screen Hustles, Grifts and Stings* (Palgrave Pivot, 2016). Amy teaches in the London Program for Tisch School of the Arts, NYU. She has previously published on *Champagne* in *Hitchcock Annual* 18 (2013).